Property of

Edward

Stevens Jr.

Latin American Issues ESSAYS AND COMMENTS

LATIN AMERICAN ISSUES ESSAYS AND COMMENTS

EDITED BY Albert O. Hirschman

THE TWENTIETH CENTURY FUND

NEW YORK · 1961

Published June 1961
Second printing August 1961
Third printing October 1962
Fourth printing June 1964

Library of Congress Catalog Card Number: 61–13249
Manufactured in the United States of America

FOREWORD

We have frequently been told over the past two years or so that the United States has "neglected" Latin America in the post-war period. The meaning generally given to this term is that Latin America has not shared equitably in the bounty of grants and loans which has flowed from our shores to numerous countries in Western Europe and Asia. But neglect has been Latin America's lot in a perhaps more fundamental sense: over the past years little fresh effort has been taken on our part to understand Latin America, to explore its economic, social and political problems, to begin a dialogue with its intellectuals and social scientists.

Desirous to make a modest contribution in this field, the Twentieth Century Fund organized a Latin American study group which held a number of sessions during the winter and spring of 1959–60. The group set itself the task of exploring present Latin American attitudes toward the principal economic problems that are being encountered in the area. Its members were drawn from universities and Washington agencies. Ordinarily economists, who constituted a majority of the participants, have a strong urge to sit as judges or to act as cure-prescribing doctors. But they were earnestly asked to repress this urge; for the task that the group undertook was to identify the reasons for which Latin Americans advocate, adopt and change certain economic policies, and thus to throw some light on the policy-making process. This emphasis on exploring what was called the "Latin American style" was suggested by Albert Hirschman, rapporteur of the group, who is now at work on an extended study of economic policy-making in Latin America for the Twentieth Century Fund.

With the exception of Dr. Carroll's paper on land reform, the papers which are brought together in this volume were contributed in the course of or as a result of the discussions of the study group. It will be apparent that some have retained their original informal character, while others have been considerably expanded and refined. When controversy arose, discussion papers were invited. We are particularly happy to include three contributions from Latin American authors.

The present volume cannot claim any kind of comprehensive coverage. While certain issues are explored in some detail, others are touched on quite lightly and many important topics have not been dealt with at all. Nevertheless, in view of the lack of adequate intellectual contact between this country and Latin America it was felt that publication of the volume would serve a useful purpose at this time.

AUGUST HECKSCHER, *Director*
The Twentieth Century Fund

41 East 70 Street, New York 21
March 1961

IN addition to the authors of papers here included, the following were members of the study group:

JOHN H. ADLER, Economic Adviser, International Bank for Reconstruction and Development

GERALD M. ALTER, Economic Adviser, International Bank for Reconstruction and Development

REYNOLD E. CARLSON, Professor of Economics, Vanderbilt University

VINCENT CHECCHI, Economic Consultant

PHILIP GLAESSNER, Inter-American Development Bank

CHARLES E. LINDBLOM, Professor of Economics, Yale University

CHARLES WAGLEY, Professor of Anthropology, Columbia University

ALFRED C. WOLF, Director, Latin American and Caribbean Program, Ford Foundation

CONTENTS

Latin American Issues ESSAYS AND COMMENTS

IDEOLOGIES OF ECONOMIC DEVELOPMENT IN LATIN AMERICA

by ALBERT O. HIRSCHMAN

Why is there so much wretchedness, so much poverty in this fabulous land . . . ? Ah, says one – it is the priests' fault; another blames it on the military; still others on the Indian; on the foreigner; on democracy; on dictatorship; on bookishness; on ignorance; or finally on divine punishment.

– Daniel Cosío Villegas,
Extremos de América, Tezontle,
Mexico City, 1949, p. 105

THIS paper attempts to review the principal ideas on the character of Latin America's development problems which have been and are being put forward by Latin American writers and social scientists.[1] Such an undertaking, if at all successful, will be more than a contribution to the history of ideas.

1. The term "ideology" (of economic development) is used here, without derogatory connotation, to designate any moderately consistent body of beliefs, ideas or propositions, tested or untested, that aims at explaining Latin America's economic backwardness and at indicating its cure.

Albert O. Hirschman is Professor of International Economic Relations at Columbia University. *An earlier draft of this paper was submitted to the Subcommittee on Latin America of the Committee for Economic Development (CED). The author is grateful to Henry Aubrey, Amitai Etzioni, Federico Herschel, Lincoln Gordon and Joseph Grunwald for valuable critical comments.*

We need not go all the way with Keynes' dictum that "the world is ruled by little else" than by the ideas, both the right and the wrong ones, of economists and political philosophers to recognize the importance of these ideas for the shaping of reality. Yet the subject is strangely neglected. We are far better informed about changes in the balance of payments, terms of trade, capital formation, etc., of foreign countries than about the climate of opinion, the alignment of contending economic theories on policy issues, or about the emergence of new reform proposals. When we are called upon to advise a Latin American country on economic policy it is only natural that, hard pressed, we should first of all attempt to get at the "facts," a difficult enough undertaking. But frequently our advice will be futile unless we have also gained *an understanding of the understanding* Latin Americans have of their own reality.

A better knowledge of Latin American economic ideas seems particularly important at this time. Rapid political and social changes in the area lead to the sudden appearance of new leaders. Without much experience in the handling of public affairs and with a strong desire quickly to solve their country's problems, they are apt to reach out for the ready-made policy prescriptions of various ideologies.

What follows is a first, tentative and very incomplete inquiry into a subject with vast and virtually unexplored possibilities. It will be possible to consider only a few central ideas that have been proposed on the cause and cure of Latin America's economic backwardness. The author hopes that his effort will stimulate others — particularly Latin Americans — to give us more systematic studies in his field.[2]

FROM INDEPENDENCE TO THE FIRST WORLD WAR: THE AGE OF SELF-INCRIMINATION

Some of the best known ideologies of economic development have arisen or have become prominent and influential in countries

2. For a survey of ideological themes encountered in "latecomers" outside of Latin America, see Mary Matossian, "Ideologies of Delayed Industrializa-

whose economic progress was seriously lagging behind that of the industrial leaders. *Relative economic backwardness* is thus an important concept which Alexander Gerschenkron has used with powerful effect to explain the specific characteristics of the successive forward surges of France, Germany and Russia in the 19th century and to show how every one of these thrusts was accompanied by a specific set of ideas about the cause and cure of the lag that was to be overcome. With respect to these countries it appears that the greater the lag the more radical and exalted were the theories which fired the effort at catching up.

Unfortunately, this suggestive generalization does not seem to hold in Latin America (or, for that matter, in the other countries which are today considered to be underdeveloped). The lag of the Latin American countries behind the industrial and general economic progress of Europe in the 19th century did not then give rise to any indigenous theories, ideas or views about the nature of Latin America's development problem. The reason may be that for many decades after the wars of independence the problems of survival, organization and consolidation of the South American states in the midst of border disputes, internal revolts and civil wars stood in the center of public attention so that the "ideologues" concentrated first on the problem of political organization.

This is not the place to retrace the development of Latin American political thought. But it should perhaps be briefly recalled that the constitutions which were adopted by the new Latin American states were largely inspired, if not copied, from that of the United States while the "generous ideas of the French Revolution" served as the ideological foundation for the new republics. With the constitutions being continually violated, suspended and rewritten by the numerous military dictators and with the actual political, social and economic conditions being extraordinarily far removed from Liberty, Equality and Fraternity, there developed in Latin America that characteristic divorce between ideology and reality which has been well characterized by Octavio Paz in his incisive essay on Mexico, *El laberinto de la soledad:*

> The liberal and democratic ideology, far from expressing our concrete historical situation, obscured it. The political lie in-

tion: Some Tensions and Ambiguities," *Economic Development and Cultural Change,* Vol. 6, April 1958, pp. 217–28.

> stalled itself almost constitutionally among our countries. The moral damage has been incalculable and reaches into deep layers of our character. Lies are something we move in with ease. During more than a hundred years we have suffered regimes of brute force, which were at the service of feudal oligarchies, but utilized the language of liberty.[3]

This permanent and painful "collision between theory and practice, between words and action, between content and form"[4] has been described by virtually all observers of the Latin American scene and we shall see that, far from dead, it has invaded new territories, such as economic and social policy-making.

The inability of the political system to provide basic requisites of law and order, the spectacle of the strides made by Europe and the United States and the defeats and humiliations suffered (mainly by Mexico) at the hands of the Colossus of the North did lead, in the course of the 19th century, to considerable soul-searching on the part of Latin American intellectuals. They turned away from the revolutionary ideals and dreams which had served their countries poorly and became willing to settle for less than utopia. In the second half of the century, many came to preach "a practical sense of life," "an inquiring, experimental and practical mind," "rigorous scientific method" and "clearly defined, positive ends."[5] This state of mind found its most curious expression in the ideological support many of Mexico's outstanding educators and intellectuals gave to the long dictatorship (1884–1911) of Porfirio Díaz, the "honest tyrant" who was to bring order out of chaos and prosperity out of stagnation and misery. It is well to recall that Díaz was admired not only by Mexican intellectuals; Tolstoy among others hailed him as a "modern Cromwell" who used autocratic methods in guiding his country toward democracy.[6] Thus, under Porfirio Díaz, Mexico experimented with an idea that today has wide currency and application in the Middle East and Asia:

3. Second edition, Fondo de Cultura Económica, Mexico, 1959, pp. 110–11.
4. J. F. Normano, *The Struggle for South America,* Boston and New York, 1931, p. 206.
5. Leopoldo Zea, "Positivism and Porfirism in Latin America," in *Ideological Differences and World Order,* F. S. C. Northrop, ed., Yale University Press, New Haven, 1949, p. 170.
6. Quoted in C. O. Bunge, *Nuestra América,* 6th edition, Buenos Aires, 1918, pp. 309–10.

namely, that one-man military rule can play a positive, tutelary role in a new country by ridding it of corruption, by giving it a vacation from disruptive political strife, and by guiding it firmly and efficiently toward modernity.

One reason why educators such as Justo Sierra threw their support to Díaz was their strong feeling that much time and patient work was needed to remedy Mexico's ills. Indeed, faced with the incapacity of Latin American societies to achieve stable, just and progressive government, they concluded that nothing less than a complete transformation of Latin American "character" and society was required and this was evidently a long-term task. The structure of society was to be improved through the formation of a middle class and patient education was needed thoroughly to reshape the Latin American character.

In this latter respect, feelings ran to an astonishingly high pitch. At the beginning of this century, some of the most widely read works by Latin Americans about themselves and their society consisted of little more than a seemingly endless and remarkably pitiless recitation of their vices and failures. Outstanding among these works were Bunge's *Nuestra América*[7] and Bomfim's *O parasitismo social e evolução: A América Latina* (Rio de Janeiro, 1903). Strongly influenced by the then fashionable determinism based on race and heredity, both books barely stop short of proclaiming the irreparable racial inferiority and progressive degeneration of all Latin America. Bunge's work, which is highly entertaining and which went through six editions, contains many valuable insights and in particular a masterful portrait of the *cacique*, but his whole analysis is built on the proposition that the three basic constituents of the Latin American character are laziness, sadness and arrogance![8]

Another highly interesting work in this category which deals specifically with economics is *Nuestra inferioridad económica: Sus*

7. *Op. cit.* The first edition was published in 1903.

8. Another and an extreme example of this literature is *Pueblo enfermo* by the Bolivian Alcides Arguedas (Barcelona, 1910, 2nd edition). In his famous epic *Os sertões* (1902), Euclides da Cunha celebrated the way of life of the rugged *sertanejo*, the man of the backlands of Northeastern Brazil; but even he repeated the consensus of contemporary opinion that mixing of the races means degeneracy. Cf. the English translation of the work under the title *Rebellion in the Backlands*, University of Chicago Press, Chicago, 1944, p. 84 f.

causas, sus consecuencias (Santiago, 1912) by the Chilean historian Francisco Encina. To him the principal reasons for the inadequate progress of Chile's economy are certain pervasive character traits such as lack of initiative, of perseverance and of morality, inability to cooperate, ostentatiousness, etc. These traits, in turn, are due to poor heredity and the wrong kind of education.[9]

Today, when we are more aware of the hypersensitive nationalism sometimes encountered in Latin America, it is worth while to recall this extraordinary orgy of self-denigration, self-laceration and pessimism which can be traced back to Simón Bolívar and to his famous statement that in Latin America "treaties are pieces of paper, constitutions are books, elections are fights, liberty is anarchy and life a torment."

How was this "sick continent" and this "ill people" to be cured? The Argentinians Sarmiento and Alberdi, writing respectively in the middle and late 19th century, advised imitation of the U. S. model. Sarmiento wrote: "Let us achieve the stage of development of the United States. Let us be the United States."[10] Alberdi gave much the same advice several decades later: "In economics even more than in politics the best example for Americans to follow is America herself. In economics North America is the great model for South America."[11]

But the economic doctrines that were prevalent among the more prominent Latin American writers on social and economic affairs were even more strongly influenced by the British free trade and

9. Encina has some surprisingly "modern" things to say. Thus he stresses the importance of entrepreneurship and employee morality as opposed to that of capital:

"One frequently talks of business opportunities blocked by lack of capital; more numerous are those that fail to be utilized because of the lack of entrepreneurs and even more numerous those whose realization is impossible because of the incompetence and immorality of the employees." (p. 98)

Moreover, Encina probably ought to be recognized as the original discoverer of the "demonstration effect," which is dealt with at length. To quote just two sentences:

"Observation shows that in a weak economy penetrated by a strong one, the capacity to consume increases more rapidly than the capacity to produce . . . the desires to consume are communicated by imitation far more rapidly than the propensity to produce." (pp. 157–58)

10. Quoted in J. F. Normano, *op. cit.*, pp. 208–09.

11. J. B. Alberdi, *Escritos póstumos*, Vol. I, *Estudios económicos*, Buenos Aires, 1895, p. 522.

non-interventionist doctrines. Perhaps the successive governments were either too weak or too tyrannical for anyone to think of advising that they take on additional functions. Also, as Celso Furtado suggests, Latin American 19th century writers had their social roots among the large landholders and slaveowners and may therefore have shown little interest in building up a manufacturing establishment.[12] In this context it becomes significant that Alberdi failed to advocate industrialization for Latin America even though he hit on the idea that latecomers possess certain advantages – an idea which has been invoked elsewhere as a persuasive argument for industrialization.

> By preventing the rise of industry in her American colonies Spain benefited industrial Europe and handed to her a rich territory which now has to buy from the most advanced industrial nations. On the other hand the very backwardness of South America is an advantage. Instead of inheriting a bad industry, South America has at her disposal the most advanced European industry of the 19th century.[13]

It appears that in spite of his insight about the advantages of backwardness Alberdi is happy enough with the existing state of affairs which makes it possible for Latin America to acquire quality manufactures in Europe.

THE INTERWAR PERIOD AND THE RISE OF ANTI-IMPERIALISM

Up to the first decade of the 20th century this literature with its passionate self-criticism and its advocacy of laissez faire and a social and economic system similar to that of the advanced industrial nations was perhaps dominant. In the next phase we encounter a greater tendency to find fault with the outside world rather than with oneself. Correlatively, a search begins for specifically Latin American solutions to the area's economic problems. United States interventionism in Panama, the Caribbean and Mexico, the loss of face of Europe as a result of the First World War, and the Russian and Mexican revolutions all contributed to this change. Yet cohe-

12. Celso Furtado, *Formação econômica do Brasil*, Editôra Fundo de Cultura, Rio de Janeiro, 1959, p. 123.
13. Alberdi, *op. cit.*, p. 591.

sive theories of social and economic reform were slow to emerge. The Mexican Revolution was remarkable in that it wholly belied the Napoleonic maxim that a revolution is an idea that has found bayonets — here it was rather the revolution which found its ideas as it proceeded with varying speed and over a large number of years along its pragmatic road.

Paradoxically, the most ambitious attempt at revolutionary theorizing about Latin American society arose in a country that up to this day at least has gone through a minimum of social change: I am speaking about Peru and the writings of Haya de la Torre and Mariátegui.

Haya de la Torre formulated his thinking in the early twenties, in an intellectual climate dominated by the October Revolution. He soon felt the need to differentiate himself from orthodox communism and set out to discover the peculiar character of Latin America's problems. Thus, he considered Lenin's definition of imperialism as the last stage of capitalism and noted that for the non-industrial countries, imperialism was rather *their first* experience with capitalism. For this reason, Haya de la Torre maintained that a revolution in Latin America could not be undertaken by the weak and submerged proletariat, but must also rely on the intellectuals and the middle classes, which, according to him, were endowed with far more fighting spirit in Latin America than in Europe.

Under these conditions, the struggle must be conducted under an anti-imperialist rather than an anti-capitalist banner. Action against imperialism was the first point of Haya's five-point program, the others being: political unity of Latin America, nationalization of land and industries, internationalization of the Panama Canal, and solidarity with the oppressed people and classes everywhere. But like some of these latter points (e.g., nationalization) Haya's anti-imperialism was subject to interesting qualifications. For Haya explicitly recognized Latin America's need for foreign capital, but, so he argued, if only Latin American countries stopped competing for foreign capital, and united in an anti-imperialist coalition, they could obtain it under far more favorable conditions since capitalist countries have a compelling need to export capital:

> The naive thesis of our feudal rulers, vassals of imperialism, proclaims "every capital is good" while the antithesis of our passionate radicals says "we don't need foreign capital." The Aprista synthesis holds that as long as the present economic order lasts some capital flows are necessary and good and others unnecessary and dangerous; and that only the anti-imperialist state should control capital investment under strict conditions. The latter can be imposed in view of the compulsion to emigrate which is felt by the excess capital of the big industrial centers. *In our countries, the capitalist stage must therefore unfold under the leadership of the anti-imperialist State.*[14]

Stripped of rhetoric, this simply means that the state should exercise control over the direction of investment – a condition which is today frequently demanded by the foreign (e.g., World Bank) capital itself, rather than imposed upon it.

Haya's search for an "Indoamerican Way" rests upon closer inspection essentially on the desire for economic development without some of the disruptions and injustices that have marked the process elsewhere:

> Why not build into our own reality "as it really is" the bases of a new economic and political organization which will accomplish the educational and constructive task of industrialism but will be free of its cruel aspects of human exploitation and national vassalage?[15]

Attribution of backwardness to imperialist exploitation, direction of economic development by the state, avoidance of the excesses that have marked the early stages of capitalist development in the West, and the community of interests of all of Latin America – these are basic ingredients of Haya's thought which as we shall see have left a deep mark on Latin American economic thinking.

A final element is the search for elements in the Indian or primitive past of Latin America that are not only worth preserving but that can be used in building a better social and economic order. Haya speaks eloquently about the dualism of the Peruvian economy and about the need to preserve and to build a new agrarian

14. Haya de la Torre, *El antiimperialismo y el APRA,* Santiago, 1936, p. 159. (Italics in the original.)
15. *Ibid.,* p. 25.

society on the collectivist tradition of the Indian economy. In the work of another influential Peruvian, the Socialist José Carlos Mariátegui (1895–1930), the preservation of the communal *ayllu* (corresponding to the Aztec-Mexican *calpulli-ejido*) and the call for its victory over the *latifundio* are principal themes.[16] Actually, U. S. anthropologists who have done field work in Peru have expressed serious doubts about the vigor of the communes and about the extent to which they still hold land in common, engage in reciprocal labor, etc.[17] Nevertheless, the continuing belief among intellectuals that it may be possible to build on the Indian past is in itself of interest. It is part of the attempt to find an "own" way to economic progress and social justice.

Whether or not the currents thus far reviewed qualify as economic theories, knowledge of this background is important to an understanding of contemporary thinking. For, essentially, the debate is still defined by two principal questions: One, where lies the responsibility for our lag? In ourselves or in the outside world which exploits us? Two, how can we make progress? By imitating others (the West or Russia) or by fashioning our own way?

THE PRESENT SCENE AND THE COMMANDING POSITION OF ECLA

The historical background which has been all too briefly sketched in the preceding pages serves to bring out the considerable change which has occurred in the discussion of Latin American economic problems during the last ten years: While economic ideas have previously had to be gleaned from political writings or from general essays on Latin American society, we now possess a voluminous literature dealing exclusively with Latin America's economic problems. By all odds, the central body of this literature is represented by the writings of the United Nations Economic Commission for Latin America (ECLA).

ECLA was organized in 1948 as a regional commission of the

16. José Carlos Mariátegui, *Siete ensayos de interpretación de la realidad peruana*, Editorial Universitaria, Santiago, 1955; cf. the essay "El problema de la tierra," pp. 35–76.

17. Cf. Richard W. Patch, "How Communal Are the Communities?" American Universities Field Staff Report, New York, 1959.

United Nations with its seat in Santiago, Chile. Its members are the twenty Latin American countries, the United States and the three European countries with possessions in the Western Hemisphere — Great Britain, France and the Netherlands. While its membership is thus wider than that of the Organization of American States with its twenty-one Western Hemisphere governments, it has, in reality, become much more a strictly Latin American affair than the OAS; unlike the latter, it has been able to avoid an undue dispersion of its activities and has largely achieved its objective of being considered as the recognized spokesman for Latin America's economic development.

The arresting feature of ECLA is that it possesses attributes not frequently encountered in large international organizations: a cohesive personality which evokes loyalty from the staff, and a set of distinctive beliefs, principles and attitudes, in brief an ideology, which is highly influential among Latin American intellectuals and policymakers. To a considerable degree, this achievement is due to ECLA's director, Dr. Raúl Prebisch, who, in 1949, while not yet heading the organization (he was appointed Executive Secretary in 1950), wrote that veritable ECLA manifesto, *The Economic Development of Latin America and Its Principal Problems* (United Nations, 1950).

Before the principal thesis of this brochure is examined, it is useful to point out briefly that ECLA's twelve-year history can be divided into approximately three phases, in accordance with changes in the central locus of its interests and activities. During the first period — to about 1953 — the ideology was forged, elaborated and tested with the help of such basic data on the Latin American economies as were being assembled; during the second period, intensive studies of individual Latin American countries were undertaken with the aim of "programming" their future economic development; and since about 1958, the principal interest of the organization has shifted to the intensive study and promotion of Latin American economic integration or cooperation, principally through the formation of a Latin American common market. It should be noted that the new interests of the organization have not superseded the old ones, but have rather resulted in an extension of its field of action.

The Elaboration of the ECLA Doctrine

> In Latin America, reality is undermining the outdated schema of the international division of labor . . . Under that schema, the specific task that fell to Latin America, as part of the periphery of the world economic system, was that of producing food and raw materials for the great industrial countries. There was no place within it for the industrialization of the new countries. It is, nevertheless, being forced upon them by events. Two world wars in a single generation and a great economic crisis between them have shown the Latin American countries their opportunities, clearly pointing the way to industrial activity.

These opening sentences of Prebisch's brochure convey its militant flavor and mark their author as another great figure in the series of outstanding political economists who have preached protection, industrialization and "catching-up" to their respective countries. In describing the plight of the "periphery" and the need for a policy of deliberate industrialization, Prebisch and ECLA[18] created and adapted a series of arguments and tools of analysis. It would be highly instructive to trace in detail the evolution of the ECLA doctrine and to relate it to Latin American political writings such as those of Haya and to Western economic theory. All that can be done here is to give a synopsis of the essential ingredients of the doctrine.

The basic emphasis is on the *asymmetry* in the relations between the "center" and the "periphery," and it is this asymmetry that traditional theory is accused of having overlooked.

1. In the first place, the *gains from trade* are not equally divided between the center and the periphery; the terms of trade are constantly moving against the primary producing countries. The empirical basis for this statement was a 1949 United Nations study of Britain's terms of trade between 1876 and 1946; an explanation of the phenomenon was sought in the alleged tendency of productivity advances to lead to wage and other factor price increases (and, therefore, constant commodity prices) in the "center," but,

18. In the following I am drawing also on ECLA's *Economic Survey of Latin America, 1949*, United Nations, 1950, Part One of which (pages 1–88) contains an elaboration of the Prebisch essay. A further development of the doctrine is in *Theoretical and Practical Problems of Economic Growth*, United Nations, E/CN 12/221, 1951. A recent reformulation is in Prebisch, "Commercial Policy in the Underdeveloped Countries," *American Economic Review*, Vol. 49, May 1959, pp. 251–73.

largely because of disguised unemployment, to commodity price declines in the periphery. This so-called Prebisch-Singer[19] thesis about the unequal distribution of productivity gains between the industrial and underdeveloped countries and the secular tendency towards a worsening of the latter's terms of trade has been hotly contested and the empirical data which the theory invoked were certainly insufficient to support so broad a generalization. Nevertheless, international price developments of recent years have given fresh support to the Prebisch-Singer views. In any event, what is important for our purposes is that ECLA found a fairly persuasive way of propounding a modern sophisticated version of the old idea that trade can be a vehicle for exploitation rather than a means of increasing welfare all-round.

2. Subsequent ECLA publications have made less of the unequal division of productivity gains and have rather directed attention to another asymmetry: that between the income elasticity of demand for imports of the center compared to that of the periphery. The former was seen as continually declining, largely because of Engels' Law,[20] whereas the latter was believed to be potentially extremely large because of the high import content of new investments and because of the demonstration effect. Thus, as income rises in the center, the percentage expenditure on imports from the periphery declines. As income rises in the periphery, however, the percentage of income that goes for imports from the center increases. This discrepancy is held to cause a recurrent tendency toward balance-of-payments difficulties and, therefore, once more toward a deterioration of the terms of trade for Latin America, at least in the absence of substantial capital imports.

3. Protection plays a different role in developed and underdeveloped countries. In the developed center it interferes with the optimal allocation of resources; but in the periphery, because of disguised unemployment in agriculture and a natural increase in population that cannot be absorbed there, protection of industry is required from the very point of view of resource allocation:

19. H. W. Singer proposed the same idea in his article, "The Distribution of Gains between Investing and Borrowing Countries," *American Economic Review*, May 1950, pp. 472–99.

20. Engels' Law states that percentage expenditure on food is on the average a decreasing function of income.

Within rather wide limits any increase in industrial output is a net addition to the total product. This argument, which has been presented in theoretically precise form by Arthur Lewis, goes considerably beyond the infant industry case for protection.

4. A corollary on which ECLA has frequently insisted is that in the periphery the impact of import restrictions is different from that in the center. In the latter, such restrictions will lead to a shrinkage of total trade, whereas in the periphery they will merely lead to a redirection of total imports, since (a) exports are what they are – the periphery exerts a negligible influence by its own purchases in the center on what the center will buy abroad; and (b) given the high and eternally unsatisfied demand for imports, the holding-back of some imports will only lead to their substitution by some others.

The preceding propositions share two characteristics. In the first place, they supply an answer to the fundamental question about the reason for Latin America's backwardness: It lies with the international trading system with which Latin America has become involved, and with the misleading free trade doctrines insofar as they have been applied. Secondly, they all point to the need for public policies designed to correct the faults of that international system through deliberate intervention: The need is for the promotion of industrialization through systematic interference with the balance of payments, i.e., through protection and import controls. Moreover, since exports cannot be relied on to provide the Latin American economies with the "engine for growth," it is necessary actively to plan and accelerate the process of import substitution, since otherwise continued economic development will run into a rigid foreign exchange barrier.

These tenets have remained deeply ingrained in all the important ECLA pronouncements. Logically enough, ECLA conceived its mission as a dual one: to alert the Latin American countries to the precariousness of their position, and to appeal for outside help to an area which was being buffeted and victimized by forces beyond its control. These preoccupations are reflected in ECLA's annual surveys, which consistently point to the dark spots in the economic picture. Even though many Latin American countries achieved considerable economic progress during the first post-war period, the successive annual reports frequently read as though things were tolerable enough until a few months ago, but have *now* started to take a definite turn for the worse. In this fashion, Latin America's situation was dramatized with the aim of stimulating both national and international action. In the latter respect, ECLA documents stressed the inadequacy and unreliability of foreign capital inflow, criticized certain of the lending policies of international institutions such as the World Bank, and proposed additional international financial facilities and agencies.[21] In 1954 a special committee appointed by the Secretariat proposed an annual foreign aid and investment target for Latin America of one billion dollars for at least ten years.[22]

The Programming Technique

While ECLA was in these various fashions acquiring a distinct and militant personality, the organization felt that it had to undertake something practical if it were to acquire a more direct influence. For this purpose, ECLA chose to interest individual Latin American governments in the detailed programming of economic development and to lend them a helping hand in this unfamiliar task. This work marks the second major phase of ECLA activity. As with the first, it also has its basic document, namely, the brochure *An Introduction to the Technique of Programming,* which was presented at the fifth session at Rio in 1953; a revised version was printed in 1955.

This brochure represents an attempt to provide guidance in the drawing up of medium- and long-term aggregate and sectoral projections of economic growth on the basis of empirical knowledge and various theories that were then being rapidly accumulated by economists concerned with development problems: the projection of domestic demand in accordance with consumer budget studies; the projection of the capacity to import on the basis of an estimate of foreign markets; estimates of savings and capital-output ratios; and the application of various investment criteria and of input-output analysis. In conjunction with the set-

21. See in particular ECLA, *International Cooperation in a Latin American Development Policy,* United Nations, New York, 1954.
22. *Ibid.*

ting of a certain growth target, say a 2 per cent annual increase in per capita income, these techniques, if combined with adequate statistical information (admittedly a large "if"), can be made to trace out in detail the path which the economy appears likely to follow.

The brochure is at pains to point out that the technique does not imply anything with respect to the extent of "rigid state control of the economy." It does imply, however, that without state action to call forth the correct amount of investment and to direct it into the proper channels, the Latin American economies would make numerous wrong decisions; they would choose too much consumption and too little investment, too much export promotion and too little import substitution, too much investment in secondary industry and not enough in basic power and transportation facilities, too much capital-intensive technology, etc.

The "technique" has been applied by ECLA to a number of countries: Brazil, Colombia, Bolivia, Argentina, Panama and Peru. In the process, ECLA has learned much about the real conditions and problems of these countries and has contributed to the economic education of those in the countries who collaborated with the ECLA team; but in terms of actually influencing national economic development policies, this activity has been less rewarding.

At first, ECLA's studies were acquiesced in rather than actively promoted by the national governments; under these conditions and since the development programs drawn up by even the most highly placed official bodies have frequently remained "on paper," it is not surprising that this very fate has befallen most of the ECLA-sponsored programs. In the most recent country studies, those of Panama and Peru, local governmental agencies have cooperated more intimately with the ECLA teams, and ECLA is now also extending some direct technical assistance to governmental planning agencies, as recently in Colombia, Bolivia and Cuba. But the fundamental problem which faced ECLA in this phase of its effort was not so much that of cooperation with the governmental agencies in charge of development planning, but the question whether development planning of the kind pursued by ECLA was felt to be a compelling need by the principal policy-making officials. ECLA itself expressed some doubts on the subject in a study on Bolivia:

> Programming is not entirely the task of experts in the central organizations; it also requires the collaboration of public and private technical and economic offices. . . . without energetic support of the highest policy circles . . . it is difficult for the programming authorities to carry out their work. This is not only a question of status. In Bolivia, as well as in other countries, the National Commission for Coordination and Planning or its equivalent is placed at the highest level, but it still cannot be said to have received whole-hearted official support. What is chiefly required is the "will to plan" on the part of the supreme political authorities. . . . Certain factors appear to have militated against this spirit.[23]

Thus, the "programming" activity of ECLA was not without its frustrations, and it is probably being pursued at the present time with a somewhat diminished ardor, the more so since a new and powerful interest has arisen for ECLA: the Latin American Common Market.

The Latin American Common Market

As early as in his 1949 "manifesto," Prebisch pointed out that one limitation to industrial growth was "the present division of markets, with its consequent inefficiency" and that this obstacle "could be overcome by the combined efforts" of the Latin American countries (p. 47). In the early fifties ECLA compiled a study of inter-Latin American trade, and its Mexico branch was entrusted with technical assistance for the economic integration program which was being undertaken by the five Central American republics. The fairly satisfactory experience with this program was one of the elements that in 1958 rather suddenly moved the Common Market into the forefront of ECLA's activities. Other factors were: perhaps, as already mentioned, some feeling of frustration over what was being achieved with "programming"; certainly the establishment of the European Economic Community, with the example it provided and the threat it posed for some of Latin America's export products; and the fact that even in some of the bigger countries industrialization was reaching a stage at which a fairly large number of industries could best be established if they could count, at least initially, on some export markets.

23. "The Economic Development of Bolivia," *Economic Bulletin for Latin America*, October 1957, p. 44.

In making the case for closer economic integration in Latin America, ECLA relied on some of its earlier analyses. According to its projections, so it argued, Latin American exports could not possibly expand as fast in the next fifteen years as would be required to maintain the present ratio of imports to national income; and the only way, therefore, in which economic progress could be maintained would be by intensifying the import substitution process. Given the industries which have to be developed, primarily in capital goods, such an expansion can only be achieved if industrialization is no longer pursued and "duplicated" within twenty "watertight compartments."[24]

In ECLA's thinking the Common Market is thus primarily required to avert a disastrous slowdown in Latin America's economic growth rather than as a means to improve economic efficiency, organization and policy; among the possible arguments in favor of the Common Market, little attention is given to the advantages of continent-wide competition for some of Latin America's young, yet already run-down or poorly run industries, or of the check which economic integration might constitute for unwise national economic policies.

The ECLA proposals and their influence on the emergence of the Montevideo treaty for a Latin American Common Market are described in some detail elsewhere in this volume.

The Direction of ECLA Influence

The foregoing summary makes it clear that ECLA, while it has transferred the principal center of its activity from one area to another as it ran into difficulties or decreasing returns, has maintained the identity of its personality throughout these shifts.

The "ECLA doctrine" has essentially consisted in assuming a critical and militant attitude toward the industrial "center" on behalf of the underdeveloped "periphery" and in calling upon the governments of the latter to undertake new responsibilities in the promotion of economic development. In doing so ECLA gave expression and direction to feelings that are diffuse among important intellectual and middle-class circles in Latin America: first, to various resentments against the United States and in particular to

24. *The Influence of the Common Market on the Economic Development of Latin America,* April 1959, E/CN.12/C.1/13.

the suspicion of exploitation; and, second, to the idea that the cure for society's ills lies in empowering the state to deal with them. But while ECLA has mirrored these basic emotions, it has also controlled them, and has progressively turned them to increasingly constructive tasks, such as the detailed study of national economic structures and inter-Latin American economic cooperation.

To perceive the specific direction in which ECLA has exercised its influence, it is useful to realize which are the areas where ECLA has not brought a particularly intensive effort to bear. Thus, while the need for import substitution has been a constant theme, the possibilities of promoting new or traditional exports have not received similar emphasis. Industries which are to be established or substantially expanded, such as iron and steel, or pulp and paper, have been intensively studied, but the efficiency of industries which already exist has received scant attention, except for an excellent but isolated early report on the productivity of the textile industry in four Latin American countries. Problems such as those of agrarian reform and social security (not to speak of excessive military expenditures) have been shunned, partly because ECLA could not afford to prod and antagonize its members in these highly sensitive areas; partly, perhaps, because they were felt to be in the area of competence of other international agencies: the Food and Agriculture Organization and United Nations headquarters for agrarian reform[25] and the International Labor Office and the Organization of American States for social security.

In discussing the problem of inflation, ECLA has stressed various "structural" factors responsible for inflationary pressures, and has been skeptical of the "orthodox" remedies of fiscal-monetary retrenchments and realistic exchange adjustments advocated by the International Monetary Fund.[26] With respect to the analysis of the growth process in general, ECLA is rather firmly committed to the notion that development depends primarily on the genera-

25. ECLA's 1959 *Economic Survey of Latin America* carries for the first time a short chapter on "Recent Developments in Latin American Land Reform."

26. See the contributions of Roberto Campos, David Felix and Joseph Grunwald in this volume.

tion of an adequate supply of capital, domestic and foreign. In this connection, the International Bank has on occasion been criticized for inadequate lending and overrestrictive criteria. But ECLA has not only been a claimant for new resources; it has also attempted to instruct Latin American governments and planning agencies in the best use of whatever funds they have at their disposal; the programming technique has been communicated through seminars held in all major Latin American countries to a large number of economic policy-making officials.

ECLA has undoubtedly advocated the assumption of larger economic responsibilities on the part of the national states, and eventually, perhaps, on the part of regional authorities in a variety of fields. But the principal task of government is, in ECLA's view, to give long-range direction to economic development by means of detailed plans which must be carefully laid and observed. Formulated in this way, ECLA's design has a utopian ring for societies where simple ministerial changes frequently mean total reversals of policies and where the policy-makers themselves take pride in being unpredictable. But it is this very situation that permits us better to understand ECLA's intent. Its programming activities can perhaps be interpreted as an attempt to "reform" certain inveterate traits such as the propensity to improvise, the lack of foresight, the failure ever to see the handwriting on the wall. ECLA's detailed projections where all economic sectors are made to mesh harmoniously are in a sense the 20th century equivalent of Latin America's 19th century constitutions — and are as far removed from the real world. They are a protest, both pathetic and subtle, against a reality where politicians relying on brilliant or disastrous improvisations hold sway, where decisions are taken under multiple pressures rather than in advance of a crisis and emergency situations, and where conflicts are resolved on the basis of personal considerations after the contending parties have revealed their strength in more or less open battle rather than in accordance with objective principles and scientific criteria.

Some years ago, an impressive amount of evidence was marshalled to show that the movement and style of the Bolsheviks was born out of a protest against, and a determined negation of, the Russian character and "soul" that had been popularized by the great Russian novelists of the 19th century.[27] Similarly the style that ECLA would like to implant in Latin America is perhaps born from the desire to stamp out those traditional traits which are felt to be hindrances and handicaps on the road to economic progress. Here ECLA rejoins essentially those earlier analysts of Latin American backwardness who had concluded that the Latin American character has to be thoroughly remolded before anything useful can be achieved. ECLA never says so; on the contrary, as we have seen, it has devised new arguments in support of the idea that the "periphery's" difficulties are to be blamed on the "center" — but these difficulties being taken for granted, ECLA's prescriptions are nevertheless implicitly premised on a revolutionary overhauling of the basic realities of economic policy-making in the continent.

ECLA'S CRITICS

ECLA's voice is, no doubt, the one that is heard loudest today in the debate on Latin America's economic problems, and there is little doubt that its views are representative of a large section of the new middle class. But it would be a mistake to think that its doctrines are unquestioningly accepted by all influential economic circles in Latin America. The opposition comes essentially from two different sectors: in the first place, from those who are highly skeptical of the ability of the state in Latin America to operate competently in the field of economic policy and planning; and, secondly, from those who simply dissent in various other ways from ECLA's diagnosis and emphasis.

Distrust of the State's Capabilities

For many Latin Americans, the state has so thoroughly demonstrated its total ineptness in the discharge of economic functions that the idea of entrusting it with some sort of general staff functions in the direction of the national economy seems utterly ludicrous to them. Their "ideological vision" is similar to that of Adam Smith, who, as Schumpeter said, felt nothing but "disgust . . . at the inefficiency of the English bureaucracy and at the cor-

27. Nathan Leites, *A Study of Bolshevism,* The Free Press, Glencoe, Ill., 1953.

ruption of the politicians."[28] This kind of feeling is far more widespread in Latin America than might be supposed from a perusal of current Latin American economic writings.

It has been said, and perhaps with good reason, that the private entrepreneur does not command nearly as much prestige in underdeveloped countries where he merely "imitates" as he once enjoyed in the pioneer industrial countries where he truly innovated. But that does not mean that correspondingly more prestige is held by the state. Long experience with official corruption and incompetence has led to an attitude of distrust and contempt toward the state and a bureaucracy which has no civil service tradition and where all major as well as most minor appointments are political. Frequently the state is compared to the organized bandits of the backlands exacting their tribute and leading a purely parasitic existence. The idea that economic development takes place in spite of, rather than because of, state action is well expressed in the Brazilian saying "Our country grows by night when the politicians sleep." Even those who are anxious to have the state carry out important new functions and tasks for economic development show occasionally an awareness of the considerable difficulties of such an undertaking, difficulties arising from the bureaucratic, parasitic and "clientelistic" traditions of what is known in Brazil as the "*Cartorial* (paper-shuffling or Notarial) State."[29] The violent desire to put an end to the "*Cartorial* State" and to start afresh in an atmosphere dedicated to economic and social progress and uncontaminated by old-time *clientelismo* goes far toward explaining the move of Brazil's capital from Rio to Brasília.

The lengthy period of civil war and virtual anarchy punctuated by military dictatorship through which most of Latin America passed in the 19th century was ill-suited to create in the Latin American mind a very respectful picture of the state. During that period, a particularly confusing stretch of Colombia's history is known as the time of the "*patria boba,*" the "stupid fatherland"; and "*hacer patria,*" "to make (or build) the fatherland," denotes

28. "Science and Ideology," *American Economic Review,* Vol. 39, March 1949, p. 353.
29. Cf. Helio Jaguaribe, *O Nacionalismo na atualidade brasileira,* Instituto Superior de Estudos Brasileiros, Rio de Janeiro, 1958, pp. 41, 44.

there typically the activity not of agents of the state, but of farmers who are settling virgin territories or of engineers and entrepreneurs building new plants and factories. In all countries many tales are current about the utter incompetence of the state as an entrepreneur; some draw the conclusion that "better planning" is needed, but others are convinced that state-run enterprises are necessarily stillborn.

These diffuse feelings of skepticism about the state's entrepreneurial and planning abilities found, of course, particularly vigorous spokesmen in the 19th century. Thus, most of Alberdi's economic essays lead up to the moral that "there is no better or safer way to impoverish a country than to entrust its government with the task to enrich it."[30]

The depression of the thirties and the rise of Soviet power have made it impossible for the contemporary observer to be quite so trenchant, but Latin American experiences of recent years with their widespread and often misguided interventionism have nevertheless permitted some strong critics to appear on the scene, the best known of whom is perhaps Professor Eugenio Gudin of Brazil. In a discussion of the ECLA programming technique, after enumerating all the factors of uncertainty (particularly irrational governmental policies) to which economic life in Latin America is subject, Gudin writes:

> Considering all these factors . . . , to pretend to frame quantitative estimates of demand, supplies, savings, investments, sounds like discussing the sex of the angels in the midst of a serious battle . . . What the governments of these countries can do for their economic development is not programming: it is simply *not to disturb or prevent it* by indulging in such evils as political warfare, demagogy, inflation, hostility . . . to foreign capital, unbalanced or excessive protection to industry and/or agriculture, etc. If these evils can be avoided, then economic development is almost automatic; if they cannot, then economic development is doomed.[31]

We are almost back here to Adam Smith, who said: "Little else is requisite to carry a state to the highest degree of opulence from the lowest barbarism, but peace, easy taxes, and a tolerable ad-

30. *Op. cit.*, p. 544.
31. Discussion paper presented at the Rio roundtable of the International Economic Association, 1957.

ministration of justice." However, in the positive part of his paper and in other writings,[32] Professor Gudin has principally stressed the importance of agriculture (where foreign techniques cannot simply be copied), of the export sector (where underdeveloped countries are under compulsion to turn out a quality product), and of education (because of the cessation of large-scale immigration Latin America must devote more resources to education than did the United States at a corresponding stage of its history).

Sentiments similar to those of Gudin are also expressed in a recent "primer" on Colombian economic problems, written by one of Colombia's most progressive industrialists:

> In the Latin American countries there exists an important school which maintains that economic progress must necessarily be directed by the State . . . What foundation is there for such a statement? None.
>
> . . . The public should not accept blindly development plans. It must recall that bureaucracy is always interested in elaborating such plans, since they give it economic power and advantages . . .
>
> The paperwork imposed by public agencies is one of the biggest obstacles to production in Latin America . . . the state complicates the life of the citizens and it doesn't care if it makes them lose their time. It behaves with an unshakable indifference, like an occupation army in a defeated country.
>
> In Colombia the state has invested huge sums to build low-cost houses, but has accomplished nothing in spite of the money that has been spent. The reason of this failure is that the state is a very poor manager. This goes for every state and particularly the Colombian one. Now, of all economic activities the one most difficult to manage and where opportunities for thievery are greatest is that of construction. As was to be expected, the building of low-cost houses by the state has resulted in a huge destruction of national wealth.[33]

32. E.g., *Inflação*, 2nd edition, AGIR, Rio de Janeiro, 1959.

33. Hernán Echavarría Olózaga, *El sentido común en la economía colombiana*, Imprenta Nacional, Bogotá, 1958, pp. 176–77, 301, 230. It should be noted that Echavarría started his career as an economist with an exposition of Keynesian ideas. He played a prominent part in the overthrow of the Rojas Pinilla regime and was Minister of Communications in the first Lleras Cabinet. Recently he has been a strong advocate of stiffer land taxation as a means to improved land utilization and distribution.

Seldom does one find these ideas expressed so openly and candidly; their most vocal advocates are businessmen ordinarily not given to putting their opinions on paper.[34] Nevertheless, it is useful to realize the strength of these feelings of distrust toward the state's actions and capabilities; periodically they gain the upper hand in one or the other of the Latin American countries and we find ourselves surprised to deal with a Minister of Finance whose enthusiasm for the dismantling of all controls and whose aversion to public investment in industry and to development planning seem a bit hysterical and old-fashioned to us!

Policy vs. Projections

Apart from the groups which are out of sympathy with ECLA simply because its view implies what they deem to be an excessive degree of governmental intervention in the economy, there are those who oppose or criticize ECLA because they disagree with parts of the ECLA analysis and with some of its policy implications. Perhaps the most outspoken of this group of ECLA's critics is the Brazilian economist, Roberto de Oliveira Campos, who, as director of the Brazilian National Bank for Economic Development from 1955 to 1959, frequently came into close contact with ECLA. The following account of Campos' views is based on several of his papers, primarily on a memorandum he prepared for the 7th Session of ECLA at La Paz in 1957.[35] In this memorandum Campos does not criticize ECLA directly, but his emphasis is markedly different.

Campos pays the compliment to Prebisch that he has been a "creator of enthusiasms and a destroyer of illusions, tasks which are not always easy to reconcile." Evidently, he believes that Prebisch has been more successful in the former role than in the latter, for he devotes most of his paper to an analysis of the il-

34. In a recent survey among large Colombian corporations on artificial barriers to private domestic investment, the instability of governmental economic policies was mentioned most frequently by the respondents, ahead of such other factors as lack of bank credit, high taxes, etc. Cf. Eduardo Wiesner Duran, "Barreras artificiales a la inversión doméstica en la industria nacional," *Revista del Banco de la República*, Sept. 1959.

35. As published in *El Trimestre Económico*, April–June 1957, pp. 214–24. Campos has contributed an essay to the present volume which in some respects is a further elaboration of this memorandum.

lusions which the Latin American countries still have to overcome:

(1) the illusion that inflation can be used, except for brief and intermittent periods, as an instrument to increase capital formation;
(2) the illusion that merely by substituting state for private management (e.g., in public utilities) new economic resources are being created;
(3) the illusion that social progress and redistribution of income can be legislated regardless and ahead of output and productivity gains;
(4) finally he speaks of a "mechanistic" illusion which consists in giving undue priority to industrial development in comparison with agriculture, and to physical capital in comparison with investment in education and technical skills.

In listing and commenting on these illusions, Campos probably intended to prod ECLA into giving more attention to influencing the *current* economic policies of Latin American governments. In general, his principal point of difference with ECLA appears to consist in the position that many more economic variables are subject to change through *policy* than ECLA's projections would lead one to believe. In analyzing shortages in power and transportation, he focuses less on inadequate capital formation and faulty programming than on more proximate factors such as utility and railway rate fixing policies. If export receipts are inadequate he does not proclaim an inevitable tendency toward low price and income elasticities of demand for Brazil's export products, but suggests to his own country the adoption of a realistic exchange rate and to Brazil's customers a reduction in their revenue duties and excise taxes.[36]

Campos thus is concerned with present and pressing dangers, and appears to look at problems in a pragmatic or, to use Lindblom's term, "incrementalist" way.[37] Several other Latin American

36. As one of the four experts who wrote the report *Trends in International Trade* for GATT in 1958, Campos was particularly responsible for the sections dealing with these taxes and their effect on the exports of underdeveloped countries.

37. C. E. Lindblom, "Policy Analysis," *American Economic Review*, June 1958.

economists could be similarly characterized. For the time being, they are clearly an exception on the emotion-ridden Latin American scene. But the exception is significant for it appears among those who have been wrestling with the real problems faced by economies in the process of rapid growth.

ACCOUNTING FOR RECENT GROWTH: MEXICO AND BRAZIL

Here we come to a strange gap in Latin America's economic literature: few analyses are available of the very substantial economic progress that has actually taken place in a number of Latin American countries over the past twenty years.[38] ECLA, as we have seen, has minimized this progress by stressing its precariousness and its dependence on non-recurrent windfall gains, such as the post-war improvement in Latin America's terms of trade. Actually, however, the exceptionally favorable factors appear frequently to be more than offset by such unfavorable contingencies as civil war in Colombia and inflation in Brazil. Where growth has taken place it is therefore a rather sturdy reality begging for an explanation.

On the whole, the experience of economic growth has not yet profoundly affected attitudes and certainly has not yet led to a climate in which hope and confidence have a secure place. Development is still discussed as something to be miraculously "launched" rather than something whose momentum is to be maintained. It is hard to break with the habit of fault-finding and self-recrimination. The question asked is hardly ever: How can we build on our achievements of the last ten or twenty years?[39]

The only two countries where an intellectual effort has been made to come to grips with the phenomenon of growth appear

38. Mexico and Brazil should clearly be moved up into Rostow's take-off column. The "take-off" concept, useful as it is, runs into some trouble when one tries to apply it to Latin American countries; some of them, like Argentina, appear to behave like helicopters with their ability to hover and come right down again after take-off, rather than like the conventional planes of Rostow's metaphor.

39. An exception comes to my attention as this volume goes to press: Víctor Urquidi discusses the tasks ahead for the Mexican economy against the backdrop of what he calls and convincingly documents as the Mexican economic "miracle" of the last twenty years in "Problemas fundamentales de la economía mexicana," *Cuadernos Americanos,* 1961, No. 1, pp. 69–103.

to be Mexico and Brazil. The economic development of these countries has been sufficiently sustained and conspicuous in recent decades that notice had to be taken by intellectuals, novelists, and even by economists.

To start with the latter and with Mexico, we find an interesting account of the process in a series of articles by Edmundo Flores, an agricultural economist.

According to Flores, the basis of Mexico's development is the agrarian reform. It led to the

> unchaining of creative forces to which we must largely attribute the development of modern Mexico . . . The Conquest submerged the power and creative genius of the extraordinary civilizations of pre-Columbian America. The technological superiority . . . of the Conquerors dislocated violently the world of the Indian, destroyed his religion and institutions and caused a cultural and social trauma. The Indian . . . withdrew within himself and assumed an attitude of passivity and despair and retrogressed to primitive forms of living. But when he once more came to own land and to occupy a position of the first rank in national politics, the rupture healed rapidly. Within a few decades, the heritage of the Indian became an active factor in the formation of new institutions and in economic progress.[40]

In a more recent article, he returns to this theme of tracing Mexico's development almost exclusively to the Revolution and land reform.

> The Revolution . . . opened the country to overwhelming innovational forces. Mexico shed the inertia of the colonial period to enter the cosmopolitan stream of the twentieth century . . . Unwittingly the conditions for the industrial revolution had been fulfilled. The barriers to economic growth were shattered. Technological progress became a condition for survival.[41]

Later he describes the regrouping of forces that resulted from the social mobility which the Revolution brought in its wake:

> A middle class and new elite emerged. The latter was formed by the coalescence of the first and second generation of the *revolucionarios* with the avowedly conservative, but adaptable, remains of the aristocracy. As a further proof of the newly ac-

40. Edmundo Flores, "Un año de reforma agraria en Bolivia," *El Trimestre Económico,* Vol. 23, April–June 1956, p. 260.

41. Flores, "The Significance of Land-Use Changes in the Economic Development of Mexico," *Land Economics,* Vol. 35, May 1959, p. 115.

quired social fluidity the *revolucionarios* now appear in the guise of elder statesmen, bankers, industrialists, top bureaucrats and intellectuals while the old aristocracy that salvaged and later increased its urban real estate wealth has merged with the newer families bringing to them the patina of old family names.[42]

This view of the revolution as the agent of economic transformation and of circulation of the elites is also powerfully expressed in a remarkable novel by Carlos Fuentes, *La región más transparente* (Fondo de Cultura Económica, Mexico, 1958). There, a successful banker-businessman, son of a peon, tells a young intellectual, after admitting that there is still much poverty and injustice in Mexico:

> But there are also millions who could go to the schools which we, the Revolution, built for them, millions who found jobs in urban industries, millions who without 1910 would have been peons and now are skilled workers, who would have been domestic servants and now are typists with good salaries, millions who in twenty years have passed from the lower to the middle class, who have cars and use toothpaste and spend five days a year in Tecolutla or Acapulco . . . These people are the only concrete achievement of the Revolution and this was our achievement. We laid the bases of Mexican capitalism. (p. 110)

Very similar ideas are expressed by Octavio Paz in *El laberinto de la soledad:*

> Without the Revolution and its government we would not even have Mexican capitalists. In truth national capitalism is not only the natural consequence of the Revolution, but in good part it is the child and offspring of the revolutionary state. Without the distribution of land, the great public works, the state enterprises and those with "state participation," the policy of public investment, the direct and indirect subsidies to industry, and in general without the intervention of the state in the economy, our bankers and businessmen would have no opportunity to carry on their activities or perhaps they would be part of the native personnel of some foreign company.[43]

This unanimous testimony about the social mobility and general vitality imparted by the 1910 Revolution and the agrarian reform to Mexico's society and economy is impressive and it contributes

42. *Ibid.*, p. 117.
43. *Op. cit.*, pp. 161–62.

much to our understanding of the climate of opinion in that country. The stress on the continued creativity of the Revolution makes for the acceptance and even amused expectation of advances by trial and error, and for readiness to experiment in social and economic policy.

Periodically, of course, the question is being raised whether the Revolution is being betrayed, as in the following outburst of another character in Fuentes' novel:

> "I cannot bring myself to think that the only concrete result of the Mexican revolution is the formation of a new privileged class, the economic hegemony of the United States, and the paralysis of all domestic political life." (p. 273)

Nevertheless, one senses a basic confidence that the country will be able to overcome the new problems it is encountering. This confidence is enhanced by the idea that growth has become possible because of the reactivation of long-dormant indigenous forces and energies. In this manner, economic development itself appears as a realistic way, not of returning to the past, but of resuming contact with it and of thereby overcoming the traumas of Conquest and Imperialism.[44]

Naturally, the Flores-Paz-Fuentes view of Mexico's economic growth leaves unanswered our question about the mainsprings of the development process in other countries which have moved forward in the absence of any Mexican-type revolution. Flores resolves the problem rather too simply when he writes:

> Without the agrarian revolution Mexico would probably be today in a similar situation to that of contemporary Colombia, Peru or Venezuela. There would be good roads leading from ports to mines, oil wells and plantations: Industry and farming would show development along a few specific lines. One would find urban expansion, Hilton hotels, air conditioning, supermarkets, funiculars, submarines and other conspicuous innovations. Subject to distortions and with considerable lag, the economy would display in spots a semblance of technological sophistication but there would be little or no evidence of the social fluidity that accompanied the industrial growth of the advanced nations. Mexico avoided this chromium-plated dead-end because, irrespective of the deficiencies of the *ejido* and of the

44. The tension between archaism and modernism in the ideologies of developing countries such as China, India, Turkey and Egypt is well documented in the article by Matossian cited in note 2.

small-holding, massive land redistribution forced the way for concurrent social and economic improvement.[45]

However well written, this statement really is an exercise in formal, and rather dogmatic, logic. Major premise: to have "genuine" economic development, a country must go through an agrarian revolution. Minor premise: certain Latin American countries have not had an agrarian revolution. Conclusion: any development experienced by these countries must be "artificial." The validity of this verdict may be doubted. Causal sequences in economic development do not necessarily run one way only, i.e., in some situations land reform could be the result rather than the cause of industrialization and urbanization.[46] Moreover, in some conditions a postponement of land reform combined with a "squeeze" on rural groups through tax, tariff or exchange rate policies may be a more effective way of mobilizing capital for industrialization than the creation of an independent peasantry which it would be politically impossible to squeeze in the same fashion.[47]

We may note that Flores does not mention Brazil, which has not had an agrarian revolution either, but where economic growth is far too impressive a reality to be dismissed as a "chromium-plated dead-end."

In fact, another remarkable note of confidence in the economic

45. *Op. cit.*, p. 116.

46. In another article Flores shows himself well aware of this possibility. Analyzing the recent growth of Mexico City, he shows that urbanization and industrialization are not only induced by agrarian reform but can in turn act as powerful agents of agricultural change and progress. Cf. "El crecimiento de la ciudad de México: Causas y efectos económicos," *Investigación Económica*, 1959, pp. 247–81.

47. An active and instructive discussion on virtually the same point, namely, whether agrarian reform is a "prerequisite" to successful economic development, has taken place in Italy. The absence of agrarian reform during the Risorgimento has frequently been cited as the principal reason for the retardation of the country's industrialization as compared to that of other European powers; however, this viewpoint, which was originally put forward by Gramsci, has recently been attacked by Romeo, who argues, on the contrary, that the feudal organization of Italy's agriculture was of considerable help in raising the capital needed for railroad and similar basic investments in the twenty years following unification. Cf. Rosario Romeo, *Risorgimento e capitalismo*, Laterza, Bari, 1959, and Alexander Gerschenkron, "Rosario Romeo e l'accumulazione primitiva del capitale," *Rivista Storica Italiana*, Vol. 71, Dec. 1959, pp. 557–86.

prospects of Latin America has recently been sounded by the Brazilian economist Celso Furtado, who had long been associated with ECLA and was one of its principal theoreticians. Returning to Brazil and entrusted with important policy-making responsibilities there,[48] he now finds that his country is in the process of escaping from some of the dilemmas and vicious circles of underdevelopment. In an impressively optimistic paper,[49] Furtado describes how Brazil, through its industrial development in basic iron and steel, petroleum and capital goods, has "conquered decision centers" that previously were located abroad. Hence the economy's capacity to grow is no longer rigidly limited by the availability of foreign exchange, so that "the flexibility of the whole economic system shall be augmented." Similarly, "there will be no longer the dichotomy between growth with inflation or stagnation, since the two vectors in the process of capital formation – savings and investment – will be subjected to the discipline of internal decisions." The Brazilian economy, in other words, is in the process of shedding its "peripheral" character and stands a good chance of becoming a "center" in its own right.

With his assertion of confidence in Brazil's growth, Furtado complements in the important area of economics the work of Gilberto Freyre, who, almost a generation earlier, had made Brazilians aware of their unique contribution to the relations among races and social classes.[50]

As in the Mexican literature previously quoted, it becomes

48. He has been a director of the National Bank for Economic Development, in 1958–59, and was named early in 1960 to head a newly created and powerful agency for the development of the northeastern region (SUDENE).

49. Celso Furtado, "The Brazilian Economy in the Mid-Twentieth Century," paper prepared for the International Conference on Science in the Advancement of New States, Israel, 1960 (mimeographed). Some of the ideas contained in this paper are foreshadowed in the last chapter of Furtado's outstanding book, *Formação econômica do Brasil, op. cit.*

50. In a recent essay ("Toward an Appreciation of Latin America" in *The United States and Latin America*, The American Assembly, New York, 1959, pp. 52–53), Frank Tannenbaum singles out Mexico and Brazil as the two Latin American countries that have achieved "self-discovery," Mexico through its Revolution, Brazil as a result of Freyre's classic, *Masters and Slaves* (1933). If Tannenbaum is correct, the world and particularly the newly independent countries can be grateful to Brazil (and Freyre) for another significant lesson, namely, that it is possible to achieve "selfhood" otherwise than by war, revolution, or even discovery of a grandiose past.

clear in the writings of Furtado and of other commentators on Brazil's economic, social and political problems that the aim of economic development is far more than an increase in per capita incomes: it is also, and most importantly, this "conquest of decision centers," which were previously in foreign hands, and a new ability to strike out on one's own, economically, politically and intellectually. For this reason, the quest for development is also a quest for self-discovery and self-affirmation and thus comes to be indissolubly tied to a new nationalism which is so noticeable a feature of the intellectual scene in Latin America. This is particularly true in such countries as Mexico and Brazil whose pace of development has been fastest. One may almost say that the more these countries begin to resemble economically the older established industrial communities, the more they differentiate themselves from them ideologically.

CONCLUDING REMARKS

The search of Latin Americans for the cause of their continent's economic backwardness has focused successively on a number of possible explanations: on the supposedly intrinsic defects of the Latin American character, on imperialist exploitation and on being subjected to false economic doctrines, on the lack of purposeful action by the state or alternatively on excessive and arbitrary state intervention, on the deadening rigidity of the social and economic structure inherited from the Spanish Conquest, or on a combination of several of these factors. Every one of these explanations then leads naturally and logically to the espousal of certain policies and positions over a wide range of social and economic issues; in other words, each determines a "system," is part of an ideology.

With increasing frequency, we are told these days that in the West ideology is dead, that "the old passions are exhausted,"[51] that we no longer are in the "disposition to approach policy as though great ideological issues were to be decided."[52] We are no longer ready to become partisans of systems, spoiling for a fight with our opponent over the minutest issue; rather, we are now

51. Daniel Bell in *The End of Ideology,* The Free Press, Glencoe, Ill., 1960.

52. Lindblom, *op. cit.,* p. 301.

picturing ourselves as reasonable, sophisticated "incrementalists" bored with yesterday's ideological bouts.

If this is so, then we are seriously out of phase with the mood prevailing in Latin America. For, there, ideologies are in their accustomed roles, holding men in their grip, pushing them into actions that have important effects, both positive and negative, on economic growth.

Part of the mutual difficulties between Latin America and the United States may derive from this disparity. Given our present distaste for ideology, we are unwilling to grant that certain convictions which may seem naïve to us can be held with the utmost sincerity and intensity. We are unable to understand that certain propositions which we feel have long turned into half-truths are essential ingredients of the intellectual atmosphere elsewhere. In general, we are annoyed by the doctrinaires of Right and Left, and a few traces of such annoyance may well be found in this paper.

Latin Americans, on the other hand, frequently misinterpret our actions. They look for the "system" behind our policies and impute to us rigid principles which we have long decisively qualified or given up.

Mutual awareness of the disparity in intellectual climate should be helpful in mitigating such misunderstanding and frictions. This paper, incomplete and exploratory as it is, also has attempted to show that the ideologies which hold sway in Latin America frequently have considerable originality, are usually less rigid than may at first appear, and are themselves in a continuing process of adaptation to the fast changing reality. The scene we have surveyed is varied and vigorous; it is part of the vitality which today characterizes the Latin American economy and society.

APPENDIX: UNITED STATES VIEWS ON LATIN AMERICAN ECONOMIC DEVELOPMENT

How have economists and social scientists from the industrial countries reacted to the protracted difficulties of economic advance in Latin America? To ask this question is virtually to put in an order for a survey of the history of Western thought on the economic development of underdeveloped areas. We shall attempt a less ambitious task and limit this note to a few contributions which represent reactions to the Latin American views previously discussed or deal otherwise specifically or preferentially with Latin America.

The militancy of ECLA's writings and its proudly proclaimed intent to demolish "traditional" economic theory could produce the impression that it was setting out on a lonely mission. Actually, as has already been said, ECLA found itself during the past decade in the company of a large number of Western economists who were then evolving what has recently been called the "new orthodoxy" in development economics. Thus ECLA has incorporated into its writings the arguments for protection and industrialization which are easily derived from the late Ragnar Nurkse's writings on "disguised unemployment," on the "demonstration effect," and from his pessimistic outlook on future world demand for primary products. Variations on one of the most famous Prebisch themes, namely, the unequal division of the gains from trade between the center and the periphery, are found in articles and books of Hans Singer, Arthur Lewis and Gunnar Myrdal. The inadequacy of the market mechanism in allocating resources for development has been explained to us at length by Rosenstein-Rodan, Scitovsky and Tinbergen. In brief, a substantial and perhaps dominant group of Western economists shares some of ECLA's most characteristic points of view.

Naturally, the "traditional" economists, whose theories have been attacked by ECLA as wholly inapplicable to Latin American reality and as development-retarding in their policy implications, have replied to these accusations with their usual forthrightness and unshakable confidence in the fundamental correctness of the classical tradition. In a series of lectures at Rio, Jacob Viner vigorously contradicted the thesis of the intrinsic superiority of industry over agriculture which he held to be the basis of the Prebisch-ECLA doctrine as expressed in its 1949 "manifesto." He did not counsel against industrialization but he opposed the notion that Latin America's concentration on primary production was responsible for its backwardness. Rather he said: "The real problem in poor countries is not agriculture, as such, or the absence of manufactures as such, but poverty and backwardness, poor agriculture, or poor agriculture and poor manufacturing."[1] Consequently, Viner warns against the misallocation of resources which would result from state action designed to "exploit" a systematic difference in productivity between agriculture and industry which, according to him, is purely imaginary. According to ECLA and the "new orthodoxy," such a difference is caused by the existence of disguised unemployment in agriculture; consistently enough, Viner later devoted an article to a refutation of this concept.

The Prebisch-Singer thesis on the unequal division of the gains from trade between the industrial and underdeveloped countries and on the tendency of the latter's terms of trade to deteriorate has also come under considerable attack by "traditional" economists. An early critique of these theories and of the empirical evidence that was supposed to support them is in Buchanan and Ellis, *Approaches to Economic Development.*[2] A detailed rebuttal can be found in a recent lecture by Gottfried Haberler, "International Trade and Economic Development" (National Bank of Egypt, Cairo, 1959), and in a paper on "Terms of Trade and Economic Development" he presented at the Rio Roundtable of the International Economic Association in 1957 (to be published).

But apart from such counterattacks on the ECLA doctrine, what specific views have been put forward by parties outside of Latin America on the continent's development problems? The list we have to present here is surprisingly short.

1. Jacob Viner, *International Trade and Economic Development,* The Free Press, Glencoe, Ill., 1952, p. 71.
2. Twentieth Century Fund, New York, 1955, pp. 261 ff.

1. *The U. S. government.* The U. S. position on Latin American economic affairs has been undergoing a rapid and radical change since 1958. Up to that year it could be held that the U. S. government had a fairly consistent view of Latin America's best development strategy: while technical assistance was extended in such fields as health, education and agriculture and while the Export-Import Bank and the International Bank were both active in Latin America, the principal development job was expected to be done by private capital, both domestic and foreign. To stimulate the generation of domestic capital and the inflow of foreign capital, the principal task was to maintain or restore a monetary stability and a favorable investment climate; and the often-used phrase "put your house in order" referred primarily to measures that were held to be required in these two fields.[3]

Under the impact of the Nixon trip first and then of the Cuban revolution, the U. S. position on Latin American economic development has undergone a series of fundamental changes which are likely to be carried further by the new Democratic administration. The role of public lending was given enhanced recognition with the creation of the Development Loan Fund and the Inter-American Development Bank; within public lending a place was made for "soft" loans, repayable in local currencies. The United States moved cautiously in the direction of participating in agreements to stabilize prices of some of Latin America's principal export commodities. Most important, it was realized that in Latin America's "house" many elements of "disorder" were even more fundamental than price instability: there were abject living conditions in city slums, maldistribution of land, illiteracy, etc., etc. Thus a "social development" program was suddenly proposed to attack some of these social evils directly rather than rely on the general process of economic development stimulated primarily by private capital to take care of them in good time. The new U. S. position is thus remarkably eclectic; for the time being it expresses essentially a retreat from a previously held view, and a search for a new one.

3. It may be remarked that formally the Communist therapy is similar: The command is still "Put your house in order," but its meaning is: "Throw out the Yankee imperialists and their allies!" instead of "Stop the inflation and welcome private capital!"

2. Among individual commentators mention should perhaps be made first of *Simon G. Hanson,* long-time editor of the journal *Inter-American Economic Affairs* and author of a book, published in 1951, *Economic Development in Latin America.* Hanson has wide experience and knowledge of the Latin American economy, but both he and some of the principal contributors to his journal seem to have become increasingly skeptical about the possibilities of economic improvement of the area in general and of the justification of U. S. aid for this end in particular. This point of view is already in evidence in Hanson's book, whose principal thesis (pp. 4–5) is that "great economic advances can be effected in Latin America without assistance or leadership or pressure from the United States." His frequently incisive description of the shortcomings of Latin American social structure, business practices and economic policies makes his book a lineal descendant of the literature of self-incrimination, so popular at one time in Latin America, except that such a book comes, of course, with much less grace from an outsider. Hanson, like those earlier writers we mentioned, seems to be convinced that the basic failings in the Latin American social and economic structure are deeply ingrained; it is a pity that a person who clearly has a lively empathy with the reality of Latin America did not have sufficient sympathy for that continent to explore possible avenues toward change.

3. An interesting contribution to the debate on Latin America was made in 1956 by *Theodore W. Schultz* in a brochure, *The Economic Test in Latin America* (Bulletin 35, New York State School of Industrial and Labor Relations, Ithaca). After criticizing the concept of disguised unemployment and the idea that industrialization is necessarily the road to riches, he suggests that far too little attention has been paid to what he calls "non-conventional inputs," namely, the improvement in the quality of people as productive agents and in technical and managerial knowledge. Schultz thus deflects the emphasis from physical capital to "plans and budgets for education at all levels and for skills and technical competence, for study abroad, for research centers and institutes and experiment stations" (p. 74). The stress on these activities is motivated by recent research findings on the inability of the conventional, quantifiable inputs (labor, capital and land) to account for the output increases in both developed and underde-

veloped countries. To Latin Americans the stress on education should not come as a great novelty: as we have seen, at one point the only hope that Latin American observers saw for their continent was a thorough change in the character of its inhabitants through education. To some extent it is the rejection of this earlier notion which has produced the present commitment of Latin Americans to models where capital accumulation is cast in the role of prime mover.

4. The reasoning of my own book, *The Strategy of Economic Development* (Yale University Press, New Haven, 1958), is cast in general terms, but it has grown almost entirely out of my Latin American experience as I was at pains to state in the preface. I do not wish to repeat here my principal arguments, but it may be useful to explain what I conceive to be the direction of whatever influence my views may be able to exert.

Some of my main contentions could serve to reconcile the Latin Americans with their reality, to assure them that certain ubiquitous phenomena such as bottlenecks and imbalances in which they see the constantly renewed proof of their ineptness and inferiority are on the contrary inevitable concomitants and sometimes even useful stimulants of development.[4] It seems to me that Latin Americans still have not fully emerged from the stage of self-denigration; they are far too ready to issue blanket condemnations of their own ways and to escape to a dream world of ever-new laws, perfectly designed institutions or scientifically calculated plans. Frequently they do not realize how much they could learn if only they scrutinized the growth that is already taking hold here and there.[5] Instead of yearning for an unattainable simultaneous solu-

4. In discussing controversies on Brazilian monetary policy, Celso Furtado puts in a similar plea for probing into the hidden rationality of practices that are perpetually at odds with established doctrine:

"Any historian of economic ideas in Brazil will not fail to be surprised by the monotonous insistence with which one tags as an aberration and abnormality everything that happens in the country: inconvertibility, deficit financing, issuing of paper money. This secular abnormality is never studied systematically. In effect, no serious effort is ever made to understand this abnormality which, after all, was the reality within which one lived." (*Formação econômica do Brasil*, *op. cit.*, p. 190.)

5. The need for such learning has also been noted in other developing countries, as appears from the following quotation:

"There is little inclination to test against the realities of the Indian economic and social scene the basic assumptions . . . which are implicit in the

tion of their problems, they should, in my opinion, train themselves to perceive and evaluate the various possibilities of sequential decision-making and problem-solving. The Latin American reality itself suggests the sequences which are more efficient, i.e., less likely to be abortive, than others; and it points toward the technical tasks which these societies are likely to perform best and which induce learning about other, more difficult tasks. This view of economic development may enhance Latin America's confidence in its own creativity and in its ability to handle successfully its development problems.

---

present models of growth underlying India's development program. Nor is there any great pressure to bring to light the many revealing insights that can be found in recent years of actual development effort."
(Wilfred Malenbaum, *East and West in India's Development,* National Planning Association, Washington, 1959, pp. 36–37.)

THE LATIN AMERICAN STYLE AND THE NEW SOCIAL FORCES

by Víctor Alba

It is well known that Latin America is now at a characteristic level of economic development which is higher than that of the Near or the Far East, of the Maghreb or tropical Africa. It would be interesting, however, to explore whether the Latin American development sequence and the type of disequilibrium it presents forms a pattern which might be followed by other underdeveloped countries, or whether it is the product of specific circumstances peculiar to Latin America. In other words, does there exist a Latin American style of development?

But to ask this preliminary question which seems indispensable before attempting any general study of Latin American development, of its problems and possible solutions, one must first examine the political effects which the new social forces are having on the Latin American scene. Only then will it be possible to understand the position taken by economists and theorists toward the development problems.

Two Traditions

First, two powerful influences upon the economic life of Latin America must be noted:

1. The presence of a landowner's oligarchy which during all of the 19th and 20th centuries has constituted the only influential public opinion in politics and in economic decisions. This oligarchy took no interest whatsoever in the life of the country, was given to absenteeism and governed by delegation through politi-

---

Víctor Alba is a Mexican author and journalist presently residing at Washington, D. C. His paper was translated from the Spanish by Sarah Hirschman.

cal personalities rather than parties and, when these seemed threatened, through the military. The old-fashioned, garrison-type military figure of the *caudillo* stamp is the most common image of these oligarchical governments. The oligarchy still exercises some influence in the countries where the depressed classes (Indian land laborers, pauperized artisans, destitute middle classes) are still numerous. It has lost much of its power wherever the new classes (settled middle class, industrial workers) are growing in number. Nevertheless, one must always remember that in the whole continent, excluding Mexico and Bolivia, this force may have a paralyzing effect on the introduction of any new reforms.

2. The existence of a long history of state paternalism. Wherever there were Indian states before the arrival of the Spaniards, these were either theocratic states (Incas) or military states (Aztecs) where paternal aristocracy was highly systematized. The Colony, with its laws protecting the Indians, its trade monopoly, its control over emigration from the motherland, was also a system of planned paternalism. State intervention diminished during the period of Independence and during all of the 19th century, although the *caudillos* carried on the paternalistic attitude of the state – through the spreading of protectionism (at a time when the state received the greatest part of its income from customs duties) and by the fact that no budgets were prepared until well into the 19th century. But even today the habit is still to rely on the state, to consider the state responsible for the welfare of all the social groups (which in turn can exercise pressure on it), to assume that those groups are entitled to be protected and to be given a helping hand by the state. The new classes that have developed and are emerging into the public life have learned at least one lesson from the oligarchy of the past century – the state must protect them.

Myths and Panaceas

Ideologies and doctrines come easily to Latin America. The influence of Spanish culture was followed by that of the Encyclopedists, then to a lesser extent by North America; later the positivists stepped in (positivist temples are still found in Brazil), and they in turn were replaced by the Marxists. Today, finally, we have Keynes' influence. However, imported ideologies end up in the same way as immigrants: after a few years they become naturalized. Latin American positivism has little in common with that of Comte, and the Keynesian economists seem to be the fruit of a graft of Keynes onto a Marxist stem, which again could have been the result of a graft of Marxism onto a positivist stem, and so on ad infinitum. This naturalization of ideas and doctrines has a strong local flavor and this can be clearly seen also in religious matters. It takes place in an intellectual climate where, up to a few decades ago, facts were less important than wishes. Because of this climate there arose and persisted a series of myths which are accepted by everyone. I shall set forth some of these myths as they relate to the Latin American economy:

Latin America holds great potential wealth. (Mexico's shape on the map has given rise to comparison to a cornucopia.)

The tropical zones offer infinite possibilities of development.

The population increase is cause for pride and population growth should benefit the economy.

Education, and especially the basic learning of the ABC's, is indispensable to economic progress.

To increase the agricultural yield, the land should be given to those who work it.

Problems can be solved by laws.

To find a solution to an individual or group problem recourse must first be had to the state.

These myths — and they are myths, for each one of them could be disproved by figures or historical facts — have acquired the status of axioms. Few people dare to challenge them and public opinion as a whole accepts them as unquestionable truths.

Occasionally these myths generate strange collective superstitions, which are clad in scientific (I might almost say dogmatic) garb by the economists and politicians of the day. They become the panacea of the moment. In Latin America a ready-made cure is always available. Today it is industrialization, and it seems likely that in a short time it will be agrarian reform (besides those of Mexico and Bolivia, projects or studies of agrarian reforms are under way in Cuba, Ecuador, Venezuela, Colombia, Chile, Guatemala and even in Nicaragua). Prior to industrialization, foreign investment was offered as a cure-all, and before that protectionism; earlier, during the period of Independence, the elimination of monopolies and privileges of the Spanish Crown. In some countries the panacea of tomorrow may well be monetary stabilization; in others, the nationalization of industries.

The panacea of the moment is in a certain sense a general solution but applied through a specific instrument in a single field, with the hope — not always mistaken — that by transforming one aspect of the national life it will also transform the others by rebound. The change often comes, but not necessarily in the desired direction.

Two Unavowed Factors

Two important elements of the development of Latin America — or at least of the majority of the countries — are apt to be slurred over.

One is the role that corruption plays, especially at the present time, in the primitive accumulation of capital. In countries where savings are minute and national investment insignificant, corruption on a large scale — the bribery of those in power and their participation in new enterprises — plays an important role in the creation of new ventures. In the same way as one can say that Latin American imperialism, contrary to Lenin's formula, is not the last and highest stage of capitalism but rather follows Haya de la Torre's formula which regards it as the initial stage of capitalism, so its corruption in the grand manner is not a factor of economic decay but rather provides the basis for capital formation and can even become a sort of economic planning when the leaders plow back into the economy of their country the fruit of their corruption.

Another mechanism which is never mentioned, and not because people are ashamed of it as they might be of the factor described above but rather because they find it so natural that they would not think of giving it any economic importance, is the fact that the urban population, which in the last decades has grown threefold or even fivefold, remains very close to the land and keeps its roots in the countryside. This close relationship between city and country — even though the differences in physical comfort are much greater than in the more developed countries — explains certain peculiarities of the Latin American economy which are never spelled out. For instance, it explains the instability of the labor force and its lack of specialization, together with the exceptional ability of the Latin American worker to adapt himself to any occupation. It explains also the trade union movement based on personalities who are often corrupt (and even the persistence of such personalities in politics). On the other hand, it also offers an explanation for the parasitism found in the large cities. The Latin American peasant, accustomed to a very low standard of living, tends to adjust himself to the most hopeless situations and to tolerate unbelievable conditions. Finally, it explains why economic crises, unemployment, etc., have less severe repercussions in Latin America than elsewhere. The worker who loses his job can return to his village without much difficulty. Small industrialists, businessmen and even medium-sized industrialists can regard the fate of their enterprises with a certain equanimity; they know they have a sure refuge in the country, where they or their relatives hold something to fall back on or where they have invested the first profits made in the city.

The Impatience of the Patients

Although the list of traits which distinguish the development of Latin America could be enlarged, I shall add only one more general trait. We shall then have a fairly clear idea not so much of the quantitative as of the qualitative differences between Latin America and other underdeveloped areas.

I refer to the peculiar rhythm with which decisions are taken there. While it is difficult to generalize, I think one can say that Latin American problems pass through four successive stages:

(1) The problem does not exist subjectively. The problem exists but no one is preoccupied with it; no one pays much attention to those few who study it or who try to arouse some interest in it.

(2) Utopian proposals. Suddenly the problem projects itself into people's consciousness. People begin to talk about it; solutions are suggested, always radical, definitive, absolute and recognized as utopian even by those who advance them.

(3) The utopia is converted into law. The solutions, somewhat mellowed, are accepted even by those who opposed them before. The problem seems so urgent that even utopian

solutions seem possible, and in the Spanish tradition the solution takes the shape of a law or of a constitutional text.

(4) The reform of the reform. The law is not obeyed or else it is applied with excessive rigidity. Sometimes the law brings out new, unsuspected aspects of the problem. Here enters not the counter-reform but rather a reform of the reform, an adaptation of the principles to fit the reality in order better to change the latter.

At present, most of the traditional Latin American problems are in the third phase. The new problems characteristic of industrialization are in the first or at best the second phase. I believe that only the agricultural problem in Mexico has reached the fourth phase. And it is very possible that in the not too distant future a fifth phase will be added: a "hemispherization" of the problems, i.e., their discussion, study and application not as national problems but as Latin American problems. It is even possible that if the present political and economic tendencies should persist, such a hemispherization will come to be considered a new panacea.

Latin Americans, notwithstanding their "tropical" temperament (if indeed they have such a temperament), are a patient people. Possibly it is this patience, instilled for centuries, which explains the impatience that sets in when a problem reaches the fourth phase. Between the utopia and the law there may be a long hiatus. But when it becomes generally accepted that the utopia can be translated into a law, then an impatience which permits no further delays sets in. Just as a street may remain unpaved for decades but then within a few weeks, under the impetus of a few complaining residents, it gets paved, trees are planted, lights and even flowers and fountains are installed, so when a problem – even an individual and private one – enters the third phase the Latin American is anxious to bring it to its resolution without delay. This is an important economic factor.

The New Middle Class

In 1950 the Pan American Union published six volumes entitled *Data for the Study of the Middle Class in Latin America.*[1] The fact

1. *Data for the Study of the Middle Class in Latin America,* edited and assembled by Theo R. Crevena, Department of Cultural Affairs, Pan American Union, Washington, 1950–51, 6 mimeographed volumes. For this study

that an institution which is not inclined to embark on impulsive enterprises undertook to publish this work shows that the deep changes which are occurring on the Latin American scene can no longer be ignored. These changes have been multiplying in the last decade.

Until after the First World War Latin American society was strongly polarized: the lower, submerged classes, on the one hand; on the other, the oligarchical classes; and between the two a thin layer of professionals – doctors, lawyers, teachers, intellectuals, lower clergy, bureaucrats, small businessmen. But from 1919 on, at the time when in Europe the middle class was beginning to blend into the proletariat, a new type of middle class began to appear in Latin America. It was not composed exclusively of professionals, though it included many of them, but was an outgrowth of economic development. This new class is composed essentially of industrialists, businessmen, technicians (especially recently), of a bureaucracy which is more specialized than before and of the managers of important enterprises. The economic status of this upper-middle class is improving. It is coming more and more to take the place of the oligarchy as the influence of the latter diminishes. Parallel to it the traditional middle class, which we may call lower, is also developing and growing in size; its standards are becoming higher and its membership is now augmented by workers, artisans (who have been converted into semi-technicians), farmers, businessmen and industrialists of small provincial towns, low-level bureaucrats, etc. The upper-middle class exercises a considerable political influence and in a certain sense the lower class provides it with an assault force. According to Johnson the two middle classes make up 35 per cent of the population in Argentina, 30 per cent in Uruguay and Chile and 15 per cent in Mexico and Brazil.

Contrary to what was happening in Europe, the Latin American middle class was not taken in tow by the other forces, fascist or proletarian; rather, it took political initiative and exercised an

---

the following have also been used: John J. Johnson, *Political Change in Latin America: The Emergence of the Middle Sectors*, Stanford University Press, Stanford, 1959, 272 pp.; Victor Alba, "The Mexican Economy, Government Policy and Private Initiative," in *The World Today*, Royal Institute of International Affairs, November 1959.

increasingly strong economic influence. The series of what may be called "nationalist revolutionary" movements which came to power in 1944–45, then lost out, generally speaking, after 1948, to return to power in 1955–59, were the consequence of the upsurge of the middle class. The Democratic Action Party of Venezuela, the National Liberation Party of Costa Rica, the Peruvian APRA, the "Auténticos y Ortodoxos" of Cuba, the Argentine radicals, the MNR of Bolivia, the PRI of Mexico (which has remained in power since 1917 under various names), the "Colorados" of Uruguay, the radicals of Chile can all be counted in that group. Lately, a new movement, the Christian Socialists, has attracted an appreciable part of this middle class especially in Chile and Venezuela. In some countries, as in Colombia, the middle class has joined one of the oligarchical parties (the Liberal), while in others like Guatemala it has formed parties of a more revolutionary character. In many places, there is a tacit alliance between these movements and the working classes, with the result that the middle-class forces have organized trade unions which compete with the Communists. The lack of political experience of this middle class, especially in the countries which have been ruled by dictatorships, partly explains the events in Guatemala under Arbenz and in Cuba under Castro.

The economic, political, social and cultural evolution of Latin America has been strongly influenced by this middle class and will certainly be fashioned by it even more in the future. What seems to be its cementing force is its cultural unity, and possibly, if understood in broad terms, its ideological unity, rather than its economic status, which varies greatly among its members.

Some of the characteristics of this middle class are the following:

(a) It is essentially urban, even though in Mexico for instance an agricultural middle class is beginning to appear.

(b) It trusts blindly in industrialization as the means to solve all national problems and as the lever which will give the middle class a position of control in the nation's affairs.

(c) Although it advocates public education, it is in fact much more urgently interested in developing higher and professional education, though this preference is never frankly stated.

(d) It is nationalistic. Often this nationalism takes the form of anti-U. S. feelings; sometimes it takes the form of economic protectionism.
(e) It not only accepts labor unions and social legislation but trusts that they will help the development of the country.
(f) It generally advocates agrarian reform, which it believes will give new internal markets to industry.
(g) It favors public international investment over private foreign investments, which it regards with habitual suspicion.
(h) It does not oppose nationalization of basic industry, mining or public services.
(i) In general, it favors government intervention and gladly sees an increase in "dirigiste" activities.
(j) As a corollary of (i) the middle class firmly supports public investments for industrialization.
(k) It is suspicious of the army — as it always fears a possible military coup — but nevertheless there are members of the middle class that now fill various technical, non-political positions among the new generation of army officials.
(l) It shows a profound interest in the Soviet methods of development, an interest which sometimes borders on sympathy, although it shows no receptivity to Communist propaganda, especially in international affairs.
(m) Recently there has been among the middle class a strong regional feeling which has pushed it to support common-market projects, the Inter-American Bank, and would probably make it an advocate of regional agrarian reform extended to all of Latin America, as well as a supporter of a technical Latin American army combined with disarmament on the national level.
(n) Politically the middle class is democratic, liberal with socialistic tendencies, and in large part Catholic — which no longer means conservative.

In those countries which have a large proportion of Indians in their population this middle class is composed mainly of *mestizos*. This fact gives the *mestizos* a sense of superiority over the Indian part of the population but an inferiority feeling toward the foreigner, a fact which increases their nationalism. A great part of the immigrants join the middle class.

A NOTE ON INTER-AMERICAN RELATIONS

by YPSILON

IN our first discussion the view was expressed that the restless and perplexed mood of Latin America today is similar to that which characterized the United States in the thirties. The comparison is a useful one in many ways, but there is one difference that appears worthy of emphasis. That is the sense of inadequacy and dependence vis-à-vis the United States that underlies so many Latin American attitudes and reactions.

The North American people were baffled and disoriented by the onset of the 1930 Depression; they had to reconsider cherished assumptions of the nation's invulnerability and the rightness of the economic order; but by and large they never doubted that the national destiny was ultimately in their hands, that once they could see clearly which way to go they would be able to set their course independent of external help or interference. (President Hoover's view that our Depression was merely the backwash of a European crisis, which had swamped an otherwise sound and stable American economy, was not widely held.) Present-day Latin America, on the other hand, does not reflect such self-reliance.[1] And its lack – the feeling among influential Latin Americans that they are *not* really the masters of their fate – may partly account for failures to face up to and decide crucial policy issues even where domestic

1. This is not, of course, equally true of every part of Latin America. It applies much less to Mexico, for example, than to the rest of the Caribbean area, and less to the southern countries of South America than to the northwestern half of that continent. These distinctions are not brought out in the discussion that follows, not because their significance is underrated but only to avoid unduly complicating it.

Ypsilon, a member of the study group, prefers to remain unidentified because of his official connection.

decisions could in fact be controlling, and for the frequent petulance and occasional violent antagonism that is shown toward the United States.

A certain sense of frustrated helplessness has substantial justification, to be sure, in hard economic realities: the dependence of most Latin American economies on a very few export commodities; the vulnerability of these products in world markets, and the general decline in their prices over the past few years; the rise of new producers and substitutes, further weakening Latin America's market position; the preponderant importance of the United States as customer and source of capital; our domestic price support and surplus disposal policies, coupled with opposition, in general, to international commodity stabilization measures; and so on. But this basic economic theme is reinforced and complicated by political overtones that strike an even more responsive chord in Latin American popular sentiment. The emotions aroused by these latter may prevent or greatly hamper a rational attack on the very real socio-economic problems of the region – especially when such an attack requires North American cooperation.

Such attitudes are not, of course, peculiar to Latin America. They are part of the psychology of politico-economic development, of the hoped-for transition to genuine independence, all over the world. But the Latin American case presents some special complications. First is the fact that these countries threw off the colonial yoke some 140 years ago, so that a good deal of the glamor of political independence, and its value for cementing national unity, have worn off. They cannot hope, as the emerging African and Asian states perhaps still can, that the achievement of nationhood in itself will open the door to solution of their problems.

More important is the special relationship of Latin America with the United States, stemming from a complex of traditional, sentimental, strategic, economic and institutional factors. This relationship is seldom analyzed by North Americans; we tend to take it for granted or shroud it in generalities about good-neighborliness, non-intervention and Hemisphere solidarity; and anyway it occupies only a secondary place among our national and international concerns. But for most Latin American countries their association with the United States, and the ambivalent attitudes that surround it, are of central importance in domestic politics as well as international relations.

The often-used metaphor of an inter-American "family" permitted the United States to consider itself as big brother, rich uncle or even as head of the family. Historically we asserted, under the Monroe Doctrine, the right and duty to protect the junior members of the family and, under the Theodore Roosevelt corollary, to chasten them as necessary. Such an attitude was perhaps accepted in the early years, but it became increasingly galling to the junior members as the disparity of wealth and power widened, and as the United States grew more patronizing and assertive and the Latin Americans more sensitive of their lag. This sensitivity was aggravated by suspicions – contradictory but mutually reinforcing – on the one hand that North American exploitation was to blame for the slower progress of the Latin peoples, and on the other that they themselves had failed, that perhaps in some way they *were* inferior to the *gringos.*

In recent years the United States, deeply involved in the world power struggle, has been less concerned with inter-American family relations. Washington's attitude toward the Latin Americans has doubtless seemed, from their viewpoint, rather abstracted but still patronizing – as we chide them for profligacy, settle their bills at critical junctures in consideration of promises to do better in the future, and expect them to rally to the support of U. S. positions in the United Nations. The sense of North American dominance has probably lessened (although a considerable residue of resentment remains), but this gain was offset by another grievance: that the United States has allegedly betrayed the family tie by giving massive aid to outsiders, for the development of industry in Europe and Japan and competing primary production in Asia and Africa, while expecting Latin America to be satisfied with "hard" Export-Import Bank loans and an agricultural, dependent economy.

Such complaints contain a good deal of unreason and inconsistency. They are not, as a rule, clearly set forth nor do they predominate everywhere in Latin America. But undoubtedly they pervade and strongly influence political thinking in most of the Latin American countries, and pose vexatious problems for their responsible leaders and especially for U. S. policy. We are damned if we do and damned if we don't. We are expected to favor the Hemisphere nations as members of the family, bound to us by ties of history, sentiment and interest, but any really comfortable family relationship is almost impossible at this stage, given the contrast of wealth, power and outlook between the United States and the others. The balance in meetings of sovereign representatives is 1 to 20, but in every other context it swings heavily the other way. In fact, the family analogy is misleading to both sides, arousing expectations whose inevitable disappointment leads to frustration and rancor.

Solutions to this basic political-psychological problem of inter-American relations must necessarily be long-term and many-sided. Broadly speaking, they may perhaps be sought along two lines:

(a) through effective action to reduce the feeling (and of course the fact) of Latin American inferiority and dependence in relation to the United States; and

(b) through deemphasizing the *special* (by implication semi-exclusive) inter-American tie, the "family" relationship, by placing many aspects of our dealings with Latin America in a broader context.

The former approach would be pursued mainly through promoting economic development — conceiving this process less as an end in itself than as a means (1) to increase the economic strength of Latin America, in relation to the United States as well as in absolute terms; (2) to provide a channel, more acceptable and effective than political or military intervention, of constructive influence on the direction and pattern of Latin American politico-economic development; (3) to give tangible evidence of the Latin countries' importance to the United States, thereby appealing to their pride and responsibility; and (4) to underline our common interests and refute doctrinaire Marxian assumptions as to the exploitative character of our relations. It would also be served by political and economic integration among the Latin American countries, which, apart from its strictly economic merits, should be psychologically useful as a partial equalizer of U. S. preponderance.

The notion of playing down Hemisphere solidarity is more controversial; it runs counter to deep-rooted assumptions and vested interests in both North and Latin America. But the existing relationship is ambiguous and mutually frustrating. Certainly its premises and purposes need to be reexamined in the light of the changing situation and viewpoints of both parts of the Hemisphere.

The United States cannot consider reverting to its prewar attitude of Hemisphere isolation. While there is much truth in the charge that we have "neglected" Latin America, the fact remains that today the Hemisphere is only one among several spheres of responsibility and interest for the United States. Therefore we cannot expect it to remain our sphere of exclusive (or greatly preponderant) influence. There must be a certain reciprocity in these relationships, or they become intolerable.

The Latin Americans, for their part, being disappointed in our response to their claim for preferred treatment as members of the family, have come increasingly to recognize the community of their interests and viewpoints with those of other less developed countries of Asia and Africa. This consciousness works against any real politico-economic integration of the Hemisphere that would include and be led by the United States. Sovereignty, to the less developed countries, is seen as the indispensable protection against exploitation, against being permanently condemned to agricultural or prime materials production.

These trends also underline for Latin America the advantages of cultivating alternative trading partners and sources of capital and technology, and the industrial nations of Western Europe, Japan and Canada are receptive; the vulnerability of their own traditional spheres of influence, and the American penetration therein, encourage diversification of their economic interests. There is every reason for the United States to favor active participation by these other industrial countries of the Western world in the development of Latin America, provided it is conducted within a general framework of common purposes and rules of conduct — and so far as possible through common institutions — rather than in an atmosphere of commercial skirmishing. Such participation, in this framework, would ease the otherwise sharp confrontation of Latin American interests and aspirations by a Washington attitude that to them must always seem tight-fisted. The Western-oriented industrial nations may be expected to add their weight to the United States insistence on economic soundness and discipline, to moderate Latin American claims for specially favored treatment, and at the same time to give Latin Americans the psychic satisfaction of wider sympathy and patronage for their development. Thus they might usefully serve both as allies and as counterweights to the United States in dealing with the touchy development problems of the Hemisphere.

The possibility of Soviet Bloc participation in Latin American economic development would raise more difficulties. But it is unlikely that Soviet blandishments could alienate the countries of the Hemisphere provided the United States and its associates show a reasonable measure of understanding for Latin American needs, psychic as well as material, and move effectively to meet them.

To summarize: genuine political and institutional integration of the two continents, that would involve some merger of sovereignty in national organs having real powers of decision by non-unanimous vote, does not seem in the cards for the foreseeable future. It would entail unacceptable risks and strains for both the United States and Latin America. The alternative seems to be evolution of the inter-American system toward a better balanced configuration of independent members – the Latin countries grouped perhaps in fewer, stronger entities, and oriented outward to the rest of the world *as well as* northward to the United States.

What does this imply with regard to the usefulness and possible development of hemispheric institutions? They fall mainly into two categories: (a) those having *political-security* objectives (Hemisphere defense, the prevention of aggression or conciliation of disputes among the American Republics, etc.); and (b) those concerned with promotion of *economic and social development.* There are certain formal links between the two categories, but their machinery and operations are in fact largely separate. The strategic facts of life require that the United States participate in the principal security organs of the Hemisphere, but in the promotion of economic development the relationship need not be the same. For the latter function it may well be preferable to stress *Latin* American rather than *inter*-American membership in regional institutions. Such a change in emphasis should tend:

(1) to reinforce trends toward real integration of economic policies and action among the Latin American countries – as distinct from the objective, ultimately desirable but illusory for the foreseeable future, of integration for the entire Hemisphere;

(2) to encourage the Latin Americans to deal realistically with those economic problems that *are* within their control, rather than concentrate attention on those whose solution lies largely with the industrial nations or, in the inter-American context, exclusively with the United States;
(3) to bring the latter problems – international investment, technical and financial aid, commodity stabilization, etc. – into a forum (or, better, an organized institutional framework) in which the other countries vitally concerned – Europeans on the one hand, Asians and Africans on the other – are represented;
(4) to minimize the implication that Latin America is a United States preserve; and
(5) thereby to create a generally more secure and favorable atmosphere for our economic joint development effort.

This is not to imply that we should be any less friends and good neighbors with Latin America; but in international as well as personal relations there is truth in the maxim that "good fences make good neighbors," especially when there is great disparity of wealth and strength between them.

ABRAZO vs. COEXISTENCE: COMMENTS ON YPSILON'S PAPER

by Albert O. Hirschman

The most provocative idea of Ypsilon's paper is his proposal to "deemphasize the inter-American tie" and to concentrate on the building up of Latin American, rather than inter-American, institutions. The proposal is made, *nota bene,* as a means to *improve* relations between Latin America and the United

States; in effect, he seems to say, we will get along better if we frankly recognize and assert our separateness from one another instead of straining to live under the same roof and to make a great show of friendliness and harmony.

To support his point of view Ypsilon cites above all the fact that Latin America is only one of several areas of the world in which the United States takes a preeminent interest; under these circumstances, we cannot expect Latin Americans to maintain an exclusive or preferential tie with us. It can be argued, indeed, that the United States would gain much, not only from a deemphasis of the inter-American relationship, from a damper on the hollow phraseology of hemispheric solidarity, but that we should welcome a decrease in our involvement in the Latin American scene. The fact is that our position of power in the area is not at all commensurate with the high degree of involvement in its economic life. As a result, we are clearly getting the worst of both worlds: the degree of control and influence we exercise is in fact quite limited, yet we get blamed for whatever goes wrong. Thus there may be much to be said, from a purely selfish point of view, for encouraging greater contacts of the Latin American countries with each other, and with third countries.

But the case for separateness goes deeper. As all developing nations, but perhaps more so because of their geographical position and the claims of the "Spirit of Pan-Americanism," the Latin American countries find themselves faced with a dilemma: on the one hand, they wish to industrialize and modernize, hence, they have to and wish to become more like us in many respects; but this means precisely that they must strive at the same time for some countervailing differentiation from us if they are to maintain or acquire a sense of their own individuality. Accordingly, the more successful are their efforts at development and modernization, the stronger their desire for self-assertion, at least outside of the realm of technology, is likely to become.

It follows that if we want Latin American development, we must learn to live with this correlative drive toward self-assertion. Yet, to respect and value "otherness" seems to be one of the basic difficulties in our relations with "others." We practically have to be told to our faces that we are good only to be buried before we recognize otherness and give up the "conviction that once we become acquainted with people throughout the world, we will discover that they are basically the same as we: reasonable people, that is, who, when we have explained our basic concepts and value systems to them will warmly embrace our way of life." This "sentimental one-worldism [which] has made basic understanding and cooperation so elusive"[1] has, strangely enough, become even more entrenched as a result of the presence of the Soviet Bloc: here we have a group of countries with which we accept to have *nothing* in common; therefore, so we conclude all too easily, in the "free world" there ought to be *total* accord on ideals and objectives. Just because we have resigned ourselves to mere coexistence with the Soviet Bloc, we expect to live with everyone else in the intimacy of shared goals and agreed values.

Actually, of course, coexistence may be an excellent term for the relations at which we should realistically aim with many countries *outside* the Soviet Bloc. The difficult stage of development through which they are passing may require that their position toward us be distant and reserved and that the solutions to their problems be emphatically different from ours. It is a measure of our naïveté that Nixon's proposal upon his return from Latin America – let us "have an 'abrazo' for democratic leaders but a formal handshake for dictators"[2] – was hailed as a tremendous advance in our thinking about United States–Latin American relations. It did not occur to anyone, it seems, that the "democratic leaders" might not particularly care for our *abrazo,* that, in the particular atmosphere of nationalistic exaltation in which these leaders frequently come to power, they might even fear it as a kiss of death, since their political appeal may in part rest on their *not* being embraced by us.

It may be mentioned in passing that our striving for consensus and full-blown understanding results naturally enough in the opposite emotion after it has been repeatedly rebuffed. Accordingly we have today in the United States a not negligible group of scholars and Latin American specialists who have become disgruntled and hostile to their very area of specialization – always a sad spectacle.

A further unpleasant result of our insistence to achieve a full

1. F. B. Pike, ed., *Freedom and Reform in Latin America,* University of Notre Dame Press, Notre Dame, Ind., 1959, Introduction, p. 14.

2. This proposal was later reaffirmed in Milton Eisenhower's Report to the President of December 27, 1958, Dept. of State Publication 6769, p. 15.

consensus with others who are just as insistent on not agreeing with us is that we drive them toward more and more extreme and hostile positions. Our very reasonableness and eagerness to understand may drive others to unreasonableness and eagerness to offend. We must at least consider the hypothesis that others disagree with us not because either their or our thought processes have been imperfect, but because they attach a positive value to disagreement with us. Wherever this is so a successful attempt on our part to eradicate the disagreement (with respect to one issue) can only lead to it popping up somewhere else, probably in more virulent form. In general, aggressive and offensive behavior may at times be resorted to in order to fend off an unwelcome embrace and would not be indulged in if we were not such determined suitors.

A corollary of our position is that it may be ill-advised to advertise Puerto Rico as the model Latin Americans ought to study, meditate and imitate. Puerto Rico's advances are impressive indeed, but are likely to be discounted because it can never be conclusively proved that its economic progress has not been bought at a price in national independence which other Latin Americans are unwilling to pay. Let us note that they would thus reject the lessons of Puerto Rican development for reasons very similar to those for which we ourselves urge them not to pay any attention to the undoubted economic gains of countries in the Soviet orbit.

But the most important reason for which I would strongly support a lessening of the emphasis on inter-American solidarity is that in this fashion we would actually increase the range of practical cooperation in problem-solving activities between the United States and Latin America. Our present image of hemispheric relations is that we share quite a few basic values and that we can gradually achieve agreement on others provided we are all reasonable and progressive; and our programs of technical and financial assistance are presumed to be based on this kind of consensus. But this image is largely a fiction: the United States and the Latin American countries are not undertaking a series of joint actions because they pursue well-defined and fully shared goals; rather, ties may be established and strengthened as we jointly engage in common programs in the course of which we may be pursuing quite different goals, at least initially.

A frank recognition of this situation may help to enlarge considerably the area of cooperation and the number of problems we can tackle through joint efforts: there is no need to have a consensus on the value of the price system as a mechanism for allocating resources in order to take certain common and common-sense steps to deal with clearly excessive fluctuations of commodity prices. There is no need to agree on comprehensive development plans in order to support a wide variety of obviously useful and productive projects. The United States need not and should not withdraw its support from a common market in Latin America because it feels that some Latin American supporters of the common market have objectives that are anathema to us. In these and many other fields, instead of requiring consensus and harmony at the outset, we may hope for a rapprochement of initially divergent views as a possible byproduct of common and successful action.

It is indeed on this basis that we solve many of our domestic problems. Strangely enough, in our international relations we frequently act as though we believed that political science must stop at the water's edge, a proposition that is even more untrue than the one it paraphrases.

ABRAZO vs. COEXISTENCE: FURTHER COMMENTS

by LINCOLN GORDON

IN the development of its international relationships, the United States finds itself constantly confronted with rival claims for regional loyalty, claims which it is compelled to

---

Lincoln Gordon is William Ziegler Professor of International Economic Relations at the Graduate School of Business Administration, Harvard University.

adjust to some global pattern of priorities and allocations. Put separately, the special claim for each region seems very persuasive. The Western Hemisphere sisterhood of "good neighbor" American Republics is the oldest. The Atlantic Community, linking North America and Western Europe, now possesses the most far-reaching military commitments and perhaps rests on the strongest political foundations. Among the underdeveloped countries, some voices urge priority for the Western Pacific and Southeast Asian nations, as those "most imminently in danger of Chinese aggression." Others support the case for India and Pakistan as "the great testing grounds for the race between free and Communist institutions in Asian economic development." Still others argue for the Middle East, as the "crossroads of three continents," vital to world strategy and an indispensable source of oil for the Western world. The most recent addition to the claims for top priority consideration is Africa, "the awakening continent, key to the 21st century."

In the two cases of the Atlantic and Western Hemisphere regional groupings, we are active participants and recognized by all as the leading member. Responsible and influential men of affairs have called for major further steps toward the economic and even the political integration of both these regions. Thus it has been suggested that the United States join an enlarged European Common Market, that we join a Western Hemisphere common market or free trade area, and that we develop some form of "confederation" with both the Atlantic and the Inter-American Communities.

The thrust of Ypsilon's argument is precisely in the other direction. He seeks to improve inter-American relations by strengthening Latin America, both absolutely and in relation to the United States. He also wants to alter the relationship by "deemphasizing the *special* inter-American tie, . . . by placing many aspects of our dealings with Latin America in a broader context."

The first half of his prescription will evoke little dissent. It bears an interesting family resemblance to the idea of promoting the unity of Western Europe, not only to add to its own strength but also to make it a more equal, and therefore a better, partner for the United States. The second half, however, raises more far-reaching and difficult questions. It would seem to imply that the forum for multilateral consideration of inter-American political problems be shifted from the Organization of American States to the United Nations; that multilateral investment activities be shifted from the new Inter-American Development Bank to the World Bank and its affiliated International Development Association; and perhaps that the new program for social assistance and development launched at Bogotá in 1960 be shifted to U. N. agencies concerned on a world-wide basis with problems of education, health, housing and agricultural reform. Without for a moment underrating Ypsilon's objective of removing the cant from conventional protestations of hemispheric unity, solidarity and like-mindedness — an objective even more cogently stated in Albert Hirschman's comments — one may nonetheless enter a vigorous dissent on these policy implications.

The question of special institutional arrangements for the expression of United States political, military or economic cooperation with Latin America should not be confused with the issue of exclusivity. It is indeed to the North American, as well as to the Latin American, interest that the long-standing cultural links between Europe and Latin America be paralleled once again by broader European activity in providing capital and technical assistance to Latin America. Preferential spheres of influence in the various underdeveloped regions for one or another portion of the industrialized free world would be politically dangerous for the advanced nations and economically disadvantageous for the developing ones.[1]

Nevertheless, the scope of United States action in Latin America is likely to be so much larger than that of Europe or Japan that the difference of degree may be reflected in a difference of institutional kind. Europe and Japan may well conduct their relations with Latin America through bilateral or general United Nations action; but for the role of the United States, special Western Hemisphere institutions seem almost indispensable.

Nor is the objective of closer inter-Latin American integration inconsistent with the maintenance or improvement of institutions for Western Hemisphere cooperation. Except with respect to Central America, one's imagination is strained by Ypsilon's concept of the Latin countries being "grouped perhaps in fewer, stronger en-

1. For some expansion of this point, see my article on "Economic Regionalism Reconsidered," *World Politics*, January 1961.

tities," presumably meaning sub-regional confederations of one type or another. But the idea of closer Latin American integration through free trade area or customs union arrangements not including the United States, and through other forms of cultural and economic cooperation, is eminently desirable. It would be a great misfortune if the degree of permissible inter-Latin American cohesion were to be watered down to the maximum that the United States was prepared to accept on its own behalf.

The affirmative grounds for favoring differentiated Western Hemisphere institutions for political and economic cooperation are that the United States does have a "special" relationship with Latin America, rooted in a checkered history but just now showing signs of maturing into an intensive joint effort for accelerated Latin American development. Culturally and ideologically, this special relationship reflects a community of outlook less close than that between the United States and northwestern Europe, but not far different from that between the United States and southern Europe and certainly far closer than with the non-Western cultures of Asia and Africa.

As to development policy, the relatively favorable endowment of natural resources, at least in the southern continent, the already important nuclei of industrialization, the gradual strengthening of the middle class and the development of a lively, if often undisciplined, group of entrepreneurs, all give hope that a well-conceived cooperative effort might, in a mere decade or so, bring the great bulk of Latin America into economic step with the modern world. It is this special set of opportunities, rather than the mere accidents of geographical propinquity (which is hardly very great for southern South America) or the negative fear of communism or *fidelismo,* which really justifies a special form of Latin American development effort, not at the expense of, but in addition to what may be done elsewhere in the world.

Certain aspects of this effort simply cannot be accomplished through bilateral relationships. If structural social and economic reforms are to be accomplished without violent revolution, some means will be required to promote land and tax reform, effective economic development programming, and the tackling of such thorny social issues as the unassimilated Indian populations. A multilateral mediating body is essential to assist in this process –

a body composed primarily of Latin Americans but including United States participation. The World Bank and the International Monetary Fund are ineligible because they are dominated by North Americans and Europeans and are widely regarded in Latin America as mere extensions of United States policy. The United Nations agencies, compelled to distribute their efforts in accordance with global standards of equity and henceforth politically oriented toward the African and Asian continents possessing most of the General Assembly votes, are not likely to meet the requirements.

Apart from its obvious role as the largest supplier of outside funds, and without seeking exclusivity, the United States can make available through specialized Western Hemisphere institutions many of the experiences, techniques and attitudes most wanted and needed by Latin America. This is not only a question of industrial technology, although that should not be disdained. It applies equally to agricultural training and extension, to technical and vocational education at secondary and higher levels, to the organization and administration of a genuinely universal primary and secondary school system, to coordinated multi-purpose river valley development, and to a frequently forgotten richness of experience in voluntary association both for profit-making and for non-profit purposes.

The more subtle argument for "coexistence" rather than "*abrazo*" suggested by Hirschman is that we should discard the blithe assumption that we possess at present any real community of basic values with Latin America. With respect to economic development policy, he argues that we need not agree on the value of the price system, development planning or market integration in order to cooperate on specific, immediate and practical tasks. His terms imply that we may differ as much as the Soviet Union and the United States appear to differ in basic objectives, while still possibly agreeing on specific measures of arms control.

In my mind, Hirschman assumes too readily that the United States and Latin America must approach their relationship with two dogmatic sets of stereotyped economic policies, one sanctifying market prices in all circumstances and damning every form of economic planning while Latin Americans will start with exactly the opposite set of convictions. Certainly we have erred in assuming an identity of social values between Latin and North America. Differences in these values, as well as in economic conditions, will dictate differing economic arrangements and policies. But economic analysis is not a matter of taste. Distinctive Latin American art forms, literature and philosophy are to be welcomed, but there should no more be a "Latin American economics" than a Latin American physics or mathematics. The economic means best suited to attain given social ends may well be in controversy, but there is no ground for systematic alignment of Latin Americans in one school of thought and North Americans in another.

Without, therefore, "requiring consensus and harmony at the outset," I would certainly not abandon consensus and harmony as desirable and ultimately achievable goals. The more successful Latin American development is, the sooner such consensus may be forthcoming.

TWO VIEWS ON INFLATION IN LATIN AMERICA

by Roberto de Oliveira Campos

In several Latin American countries now facing problems of acute inflation, there is a sharp theoretical and policy clash between two groups which, for want of better terms, I shall call the "monetarists" and the "structuralists."

To the "monetarists," views are ascribed that are close to those imputed to the International Monetary Fund, even though several of them dissent from the IMF in many respects. The "structuralists," on the other hand, claim to have support for their views in the studies of the Economic Commission of Latin America, even though official ECLA reports do not show the fatalistic view of the inflationary process in Latin America nor the degree of scepticism toward monetary and fiscal policies that is implied in the "structuralist" view.

In a heroic oversimplification, the views of the two contending schools of thought – at least as expressed in Brazil – can be summarized as follows:

The "monetarists" hold that:

(a) Inflation has ceased to promote development and in fact has become incompatible with it; even those countries that managed to have inflation and development are now facing an acceleration of inflation and a deceleration of development;

(b) Inflation must be stopped quickly, before it degenerates into explosive tensions, and the only effective method seems

Roberto de Oliveira Campos is an economic consultant; he was formerly Director of Brazil's National Bank for Economic Development, Rio de Janeiro. He holds the rank of Ambassador in Brazil's Foreign Service.

to be the curbing of excess demand through a prudent combination of monetary and fiscal policies supplemented by international financial assistance;

(c) Most of the alleged supply inelasticities and bottlenecks are not autonomous or structural, but are caused by price and exchange rate distortions generated during the course of the inflationary process itself.

The "structuralists," on the other hand, hold that:

(a) Inflation is a natural accompaniment of growth;

(b) Inflation cannot be curbed through monetary and fiscal means without provoking unemployment or stagnation of growth because of supply rigidities;

(c) The instability of export proceeds, generating a capacity-to-import bottleneck as well as supply inelasticities inherent in the growth process, renders it impossible to curb inflation in the short run; it in fact renders desirable a *gradual* attack on inflation, except to the extent that foreign assistance becomes available to render the supply of imports more elastic.

To a certain extent the two contending views are less different than they might seem, the divergences being more of method and emphasis than of substance. There is, however, a *hard core* of dispute which centers mainly on the usefulness of monetary and fiscal policy as well as on the relationship between structural factors and the inflationary process itself.

NOTES ON THE "STRUCTURALIST" VIEW

An implicit assumption of the "structuralist" view is that a sharp distinction exists between the inflationary behavior and policies of less developed countries taken *as a group,* on the one side, and the developed countries as a group, on the other; and accordingly a separate theory is needed to account for such discrepant behavior.

This approach, as noted recently by Arthur Marget, tends to overestimate differences *between* the two groups and slur differences *within* the groups. For instance, *within* the less developed group Brazil followed expansionist monetary policies and is suffering from acute inflation. Mexico pursued more prudent monetary and fiscal policies and has had only a moderate rate of inflation. *Within* the industrialized group, France, until the recent stabilization program, followed inflationary monetary policies while Germany adhered to a conservative approach. It may be said, in this respect, that there is (or was until recently) a greater similarity of behavior between Brazil and France than between Brazil and Mexico.

In short, countries in similar stages of development and achieving comparable rates of growth had varying degrees of inflation and varying monetary experiences, depending on the set of monetary and fiscal policies they chose to adopt.

Is a new or modified theory of inflation, emphasizing supply inelasticities or bottleneck factors which are judged to be inadequately covered by the "demand-pull" or "cost-push" theory, in fact needed for the understanding of inflation in Latin America? Is there room for a "structural" theory of inflation, which would regard changes in money supply as merely passive adjustments to irresistible autonomous pressures generated by bottlenecks in the import capacity, or inelastic food supplies or institutional arrangements?

On the ground of the data and comments I have seen, this effort at theorizing would seem an exercise in "unnecessary" originality; but I am of course open to persuasion.

To naïve and unsophisticated minds like my own, a number of questions would occur immediately: Why not undertake a statistical effort to detect such correlation as may exist for different countries in Latin America, between (A) expansion of the effective money supply,[1] indicating a passive behavior of the monetary authorities, (B) rate of price inflation, (C) rate of growth in real product?

A few things would undoubtedly stand out.

(a) In the heavily inflated countries the rate of expansion in the money supply has been of such an order of magnitude (20 to 30 per cent per year) as to outstrip any realistic possibility of growth of the supply (via increases in the real domestic product plus net imports); at that rate of mone-

1. Supply of money corrected by changes in velocity; strictly speaking the relevant concept would be that of "changes in liquidity," involving not only money but also "near-money." But (a) near-money is less important in Latin America because of incipient financial markets, (b) data are not usually available on money market assets.

tary expansion no economy, even though highly developed and presumably exempted from major inelasticity or supply bottlenecks, would fail to have inflation.

(b) No clear relationship appears to exist (if anything the correlation is negative) between the rate of inflation and the rate of development. The highly inflated countries (Argentina, Chile, Bolivia) tended to stagnate; some of the low-inflation countries (Mexico, Venezuela, El Salvador, Ecuador) seem to be developing fast. For the others there is a mixed picture but it may be said tentatively that (1) where inflation coincided with rapid development, the latter can best be explained by other factors (absorption of foreign resources, improvement in the terms of trade) than by the full utilization of capacity supposedly brought about by inflation, (2) in recent periods the acceleration of inflation has coincided with a deceleration of development.

(c) The above data would give a *first hint* that the behavior of inflation in Latin America would seem to conform pretty much to what might be expected in the light of old-fashioned theories.

It might of course be argued that the above investigation would merely represent a *tautological* illustration of the inflationary process. The relevant question then would be: Why is it that the monetary authorities in Latin America find it so peculiarly difficult to behave actively and usually confine themselves to register on the liability side (money supply) all of the asset creation plans of the government sector, private sectors and net foreign balance? Several answers might suggest themselves:

(1) *Those pressures are irresistible in the process of growth.* This answer would *prima facie* be unsatisfactory as (a) some of the Latin American countries achieved high rates of growth without inflation or with moderate inflation, (b) even the overinflated countries (Brazil, Argentina) have achieved, in discontinuous periods of their history, rapid growth with nothing like their present inflation, (c) given demand pressures for governmental or private investment in development programs, it does not follow that the money supply must be passively adjusted to ratify those programs; after all, investment programs can be financed by taxes, by

foreign loans, by physical rationing of consumption, by shifts in the composition of investment, etc.

(2) *Supply inelasticities, institutional rigidities and the capacity-to-import bottleneck (pressures from the real or income side) are the active factors and monetary expansion a residual.* This line of argument would encounter the same difficulties mentioned above, namely, (a) some countries managed at times to control inflation despite bottlenecks and (b) there is no intrinsic organic reason why bottlenecks and inelasticities should be greater in Brazil and Argentina, for instance, than in Mexico or Ecuador. Again it is very difficult to resort to bottlenecks and inelasticities to explain the Argentine inflation at the beginning of the Peronist era.

The upshot of this initial statistical effort would be to bring out clearly, to my mind, that the role of old-fashioned monetary and fiscal policy is vitally important. Money factors are not residual but at the very core of the process. The inflated countries are those that choose incompatible targets.

The Role of Inelasticities and Bottlenecks

It is an underlying assumption of the "structuralist" school that such inelasticities are (a) peculiarly inherent to the growth process in Latin America, (b) autonomous and causal factors of inflation.

A visitor to ECLA in Santiago cannot help feeling that the thinking of the "structuralist" school has been affected by the peculiarities of the Chilean inflation and fell into the trap of generalizing this experience. Chile has had, I am told, almost 95 years of fairly continuous inflation; the attempts to fight it were until recently half-hearted efforts to conceal an open inflation by converting it into a *repressed inflation,* which created still more distortions than the open one. In the course of the process, price or exchange rate distortions discouraged investment in certain sectors (food production, transportation, power, exports) and bottlenecks arose; these bottlenecks now appear to have caused the inflation when they actually resulted from it. It is true that, once generated, bottlenecks may begin to play an independent causal role; and they certainly render the fight against inflation more difficult. In this sense the original *variables* have been converted into *data* of the problem; but this does not invalidate the basic distinction between *natural* bottlenecks and *induced* ones.

Structural bottlenecks indeed come to one's mind when discussing the Chilean inflation; somehow they seem much less relevant when one discusses the Mexican or Venezuelan situation. And for the Argentine inflation, only a fertile imagination would attribute a causal role to bottlenecks and food supply inelasticities; they were the result of Peronist policies (pegging of rates of public utilities and transportation, taxation of agricultural exports to subsidize industrialization, etc.) and not the causal factor of the Argentine inflation, even though they now complicate tremendously the problem of combating it.

We all recognize of course that there are *leads* and *lags* in the development process; balanced growth, *stricto sensu,* is almost a practical impossibility. But it does not mean that these need to become cumulative and self-feeding; this only happens when policies are pursued that convert self-correcting disequilibria inherent in the growth process into induced and cumulative ones.

A *model* explaining one of the possible methods of bottleneck generation could thus easily be constructed in the following fashion:

(1) Excess demand arising from the pressures in the foreign sector (wartime export surpluses not offset by unspent export taxes or by imports) led to price inflation.

(2) Attempts were made to repress inflation not by curbing general excess demand but by controlling certain key prices (basic foodstuffs, rail transport, electricity, interest rates).

(3) Private voluntary savings and investment were discouraged and replaced, after a time lag, by deficit-financed government investment.

(4) Inflation was aggravated, bottlenecks arose and "structural rigidities" were created.

On the basis of the Latin American experience it may be quite possible to demonstrate that, to a large extent, the alleged bottlenecks were originally inflation-induced, even though at a later stage they may become inflation-feeding.

(a) *Bottlenecks in transport and electricity.* In most Latin American countries (Argentina, Brazil in particular) utility rates have been congealed, or the capital base for rate determination frozen at the "historical" cost, despite rising costs. Results: (a) stoppage of investment, (b) net disinvestment, (c) bottlenecks.

(b) *Food supply.* Rather than curbing general excess demand it seems infinitely easier for governments to establish price control of basic foodstuffs leading to the following results:

— in the case of food for internal consumption:

(i) subsidization of demand for consumption, thus aggravating the price pressure;

(ii) reduction in the relative profitability (as compared with industry or the import trade, for instance) of the food production sector and consequently disincentive for investment in agriculture;

(iii) diversion of land from productive to unproductive uses.

— in the case of agricultural production for export:

(i) emergence of repressed inflation through overvalued *exchange rates* that tax export production;

(ii) manipulation of internal producers' prices by state export monopolies that tax the export sector in order to subsidize industry.

(c) *Rigidity of the savings function.* Freezing of interest rates to decrease costs for investors acts as a tax not on spenders but on savers; in many cases, legal interest rates become negative, forcing would-be savers to de-monetize their savings by investing in real estate or in foreign currency, or else to run the risk of irregular financial transactions to achieve a positive interest rate.

(d) *Import capacity bottleneck.* A prolonged inflation is obviously a powerful generator of "capacity-to-import" bottleneck. In Latin America the countries that suffer acutely from such bottlenecks are precisely those that have indulged in multiple-rate practices. And this of course is not a mere accident of fate, for various reasons.

(i) There are usually subsidized rates for certain basic or so-called "rigid" imports that are held to be important cost-of-living items (fuel, wheat) as well as for machinery and equipment for essential projects. The net result is that wasteful consumption is encouraged, there is a perverse substitution (against the competing national product or substitute product), investment demand is overstimulated by the artificial reduction of the private cost to the entrepreneur, but often with an increase in social costs to the economy as a whole.

(ii) Subsidized import rates go hand in hand with pegged rates for certain exports which thereby become subject to heavy taxation; this results in a disincentive to expansion and diversification of exports. There are of course cases when export taxes are advisable and necessary (to create stabilization funds, to correct domestic overproduction, etc.) and the multiple-rate mechanism may be a convenient and flexible technique for taxing exports. But clearly many of the Latin American countries have abused multiple-rate practices and come dangerously close to killing the hen that laid the golden eggs. (Argentina is a case in point.)

The purpose of these notes is not to deny that once supply inelasticities have been created through a long process of inflation (1) they may begin to exert a derived causal role, (2) they make the combat against inflation more difficult and painful than it need otherwise be, (3) stabilization programs may have to adjust themselves to the fact that in its initial phases the repressed inflation may have to be converted into an open one (prices in the controlled sectors being allowed to rise in order to correct previous bottleneck-creating price distortions), (4) the combat against inflation would require monetary and fiscal policies in a broad sense, including programs for a more productive reorientation of public and private investment, as well as a foreign aid component.

A Note on the Capacity-to-Import Bottleneck

It is often somewhat uncritically assumed that a limited capacity to import is an independent datum of the inflationary process in Latin America. Even though this may be true in the very short run it is important to determine to what extent it is again an "induced" bottleneck arising from deliberate policies that combined internal inflation with external overvaluation, and aimed at financing the rise of import substitution through export taxes, rather than through general taxation and other incentives; or from the lack of foresight in building up reserves in boom periods to avoid excessive import contractions in loan periods.

Practically all of the inflated Latin American countries biased their development program in an anti-export direction. That is most certainly the case in Brazil and Argentina; Chile also discouraged for a long time the expansion of copper investments, and through multiple rates, which have the effect of export taxes, discouraged diversification of exports.

Mexico and Venezuela did not indulge in development policies biased against exports and did not experience the same acute import capacity bottlenecks. Nor can the problem be assumed away simply by saying that Mexico had naturally elastic exports in the form of tourism and Venezuela enjoyed the oil and iron ore bonanza. The fact is that Venezuela might have adopted policies that would hinder investment in oil and minerals, as Brazil (in the case of minerals and oil) and Argentina (in the case of oil) managed to do rather effectively, and Mexico might not have cashed in on Brazilian and U. S. mistakes on coffee and cotton.

But even when the effect of inadequate export policies is discounted, it may well be that there is a residual bottleneck in the capacity to import. This is in fact likely to be the case whenever exports cease to be (and there is no reason why they should always be) the leading "growth" sector of the economy. In other words, it is quite conceivable that exports may tend to grow at less than the required rate, despite the adoption of rational development programs. This may be because of long-run downward terms of trade, lower income and/or price elasticities of demand for primary products, etc. (e.g., Prebisch's thesis, which may have validity in the case of certain countries and products because of the combined effect of Engels' law, technological savings in raw materials, synthetic substitutes, or an ambivalent behavior of mining concerns as exporters of raw materials in less developed countries and consumers in developed countries, etc.).

This situation in fact was envisaged in good old classical international trade theory. This "natural" as opposed to an "induced" lag in the rate of export growth as compared to the overall rate of development is indeed implicit in Cairne's time-honored theory about the stages through which a developing country's balance of payments is likely to pass. Young debtor countries are supposed to have an import surplus covered by loans; as they mature the inflow of loans is offset by debt payments; finally, they become capital exporters and develop an export surplus.

Upon those who emphasize the limitations of the capacity to import as an "original" and almost unavoidable bottleneck explaining a good part of the irresistibility of inflationary "real" pressures in Latin America rests the burden of proving that this bottleneck has not gone beyond the normally expected gap, precisely as a result of inflationary policies and anti-export-biased development programs. The severe constriction of the import capacity in Brazil and Argentina, for instance, seems to have been engineered by (a) excessive export taxation through exchange rate or price distortions, (b) misguided import substitution policy, (c) the wrong method of financing import substitution.

On the Active or Passive Behavior of the Monetary Authorities

There seems to prevail among the "structuralists," alongside an underestimation of monetary policies, a much too narrow concept of what is meant by monetary and fiscal policy.

Clearly, given pressures emerging from public expenditures, volume of investment and export volume, the monetary authorities need not act passively but may react in a number of ways. Given, for instance, an autonomous wage increase of political origin, the monetary authority may choose to allow credit expansion by a margin considerably smaller than the cost-push. In this case it will force the entrepreneur to absorb part of the cost increase, through reduction in profits, to liquidate inventories, and/or to increase productivity. Nor can it be assured that the fatal result of such measures will be unemployment and reduction in the level of real investment in industry. If the entrepreneur considers the governmental policy to be firm and irreversible he may not choose to contract employment or investment in the industry but will rather monetize real assets (real estate, buildings, etc.), liquidate "near-money" assets, or reduce personal consumption. If of course the monetary authority starts from the fatalistic assumption that the cost-push pressures cannot be resisted without unemployment or reduction in real investment, then there is no "monetary" cure for inflation. But then there is no "real," "structural" or "institutional" cure either. For the basic contradiction of the "structuralist" view seems to be that precisely because the "structuralists" emphasize the sluggishness of supply in less developed countries and the import limitations, they ought to conclude logically that the only possible effective attack on inflation would be a contraction of excess demand; precisely what the "monetarists" have advocated all along.

The research on bottlenecks is of course extremely useful for fiscal and monetary policy to play an even more useful active role; and that is the line of reconciliation between "monetarists" and "structuralists." For a lot can be done by fiscal and monetary weapons to correct bottlenecks without additional investment that would merely aggravate excess demand; this can be done simply through the alteration of price incentives and reorientation of government investment from less productive to the bottleneck sectors (shift from military expenditures to investment in agriculture). Nor can it be assumed, as many "structuralists" assume, that a reduction of the over-all investment level in the course of stabilization programs is detrimental to growth. In the first place, this reduction may be purely temporary, soon reversed by an upsurge in investment. In the second place, a better composition of investment may emerge (with the reduction of speculative investment) with a consequent improvement in the capital-output ratio, so that a lower over-all volume of investment may be compatible with an acceleration of real growth.

It remains to be seen whether this will in fact be the result of some of the stabilization programs now attempted in Latin America (Argentina and Colombia, for instance). In my view there is a fair chance that this will occur.

AN ALTERNATIVE VIEW OF THE "MONETARIST"—"STRUCTURALIST" CONTROVERSY

by DAVID FELIX

THE background of this controversy is the chronic inflation which has plagued Latin America since the late 1930's.[1] In Venezuela and pre-Castro Cuba, inflation merely paralleled the mild U. S. rate. In Mexico, Colombia and Peru, inflation decelerated in the 1950's, to a rate, however, still well above that of the United States. In the other major Latin American countries, Argentina, Brazil, Chile and Uruguay, inflation worsened after the end of the Korean War. The end of the Korean War also marked the tapering-off of the economic upsurge which had begun with World War II. Rates of growth turned downward, export prices began to sag, and by 1958 virtual stagnation of per capita income had set in in most Latin American countries.[2] During the past five years, with prodding from the International Monetary Fund and the U. S. government, Chile, Argentina, Colombia and Peru instituted anti-inflationary programs.[3] These have included tighter

1. Inflation has been an intermittent phenomenon in Latin America since the latter part of the 19th century. The inflationary upsurge of the late 1930's, however, ended a period of relative price stability during the booming 1920's and of falling prices in the early 1930's.

2. The following qualifications should be noted: Per capita income growth virtually ceased in Argentina and Chile by 1953–55. Venezuela, on the other hand, benefiting from the Suez crisis, did not slow down until 1958. Mexican per capita income growth in the 1950's, though below the 1940's, has continued at a fairly substantial rate.

3. The IMF has preached the anti-inflation gospel from its inception, but its influence in Latin America has increased in the past few years in direct

David Felix is Associate Professor of Economics at Wayne State University.

credit constraints, cuts in public expenditures, partial wage freezes, devaluation, and the repeal of various types of subsidies and direct controls. Brazil has thus far resisted IMF pressure.

The specific focus of the "monetarist"–"structuralist" controversy has been the IMF-supported anti-inflationary programs. "Monetarists" regard them as essential for reviving economic growth. Halting inflation and abolishing various direct controls and subsidies would, they believe, eliminate most of the imbalances and supply rigidities on which the "structuralists" lay such heavy stress. In other words, "monetarists" believe that there is a latent dynamism in the private sector as well as untapped possibilities for attracting substantially larger amounts of foreign investment. But to realize this potential the economies must undergo a painful but necessary anti-inflationary therapy to purge themselves of distortions and obstacles to growth induced by inflation. Price level stability and the elimination of various direct controls seems, thus, to be viewed as virtually a sufficient as well as a necessary condition for reviving economic growth. This may be inferred from the reduced relative role assigned in the programs to public investment. While the latter is expected to expand in volume over time through foreign loans and a gradual increase in tax receipts, no dramatic increase of taxes is postulated either as part of the stabilization effort or of the subsequent development effort.[4] Confidence in the latent dynamism of the private sector is also stressed in the pronouncements of key government officials, supporting business groups, editorials in the friendly press and pep talks by visiting U. S. dignitaries.[5] Finally it is implied by the fact that domestic support for the stabilization programs has come chiefly

---

proportion to the decline in the region's foreign exchange reserves. For in addition to its own ability to lend foreign exchange, the IMF's leverage has been magnified by the fact that U. S. loans to Latin America were made contingent on the borrower meeting IMF lending criteria.

4. The advisory Klein-Saks mission to the Chilean government in 1955–58 suggested increases in taxes in order to augment public investment, but its advice was ignored by the government and by the backers of the anti-inflationary program. Recently the Alessandri government has proposed tax increases partially to finance a reconstruction program in south-central Chile, which was severely damaged by the 1960 earthquake. Most of the financing, however, is expected to come from foreign loans.

5. Some supporters of the stabilization programs are probably "monetarists" *du jour*, to whom stabilization is a prerequisite for initiating large-scale development and social reform efforts. Nor are all supporters of the stabilization programs enthusiasts for full stability. In Chile, many observers suggest,

from the Rightist parties who have an ideological antipathy to large-scale planned development programs. This is not, however, to say that the "monetarists" want a free economy in the classical sense. Terms like "free enterprise" and "competition" are bandied about in Latin America even more loosely than in the United States. They presume protection against competing imports, trade association pricing, and public industrial and infrastructure investment if complementary to rather than competitive with the private sector.

The "structuralist" dispute with the "monetarists" is thus carried on at three levels. There is disagreement as to the causes of the inflation and of the efficacy of tightened credit, fiscal retrenchment and the elimination of direct controls in checking it. There is a closely related disagreement on economic development policy. Finally, there is mistrust of the Rightist sponsorship of the stabilization programs which stems from the fact that many of the "structuralists" are partisans of the parties of the Left.[6] The task of summarizing the "structuralist" position is made more difficult, moreover, by the fact that there are really various positions. "Structuralists" are more united as critics than as programmers.[7] This should be kept in mind in appraising the following effort at a synthesis.

Let us begin by putting forth the "structuralist" inflationary model in skeletal form. The setting is that of a Latin American country undergoing industrialization. The problem of identifying the countries to which the model might apply will be touched upon later.

---

the business community fears the social and economic consequences of stability more than those of a 10 to 20 per cent per annum inflation, but joins the anti-inflationary forces when, as in 1955, the inflation accelerates dangerously.

The official views on development of the IMF are not available, since the IMF missions operate as behind-the-scenes advisers and critics of programs which formally are the responsibility of each government. The mission reports which the writer has seen restricted themselves to a discussion of stabilization measures.

6. "Left" and "Right" have connotations broadly similar to their use in French politics, which means that they are ill-defined terms. Formerly, the Left began with the moderate anti-clerical parties and ranged to the Communists. The appearance of leftist Catholic parties in recent years has destroyed the correlation between anti-clericalism and social and economic radicalism.

7. This point is emphasized in Joseph Grunwald's paper on the Chilean "structuralists" which appears later in this volume.

The model has the following basic features. There is chronic upward pressure on import and food prices. These, respectively, raise domestic costs and set off wage demands, culminating in a general rise of the cost-price level, with oligopoly pricing in industry and trade facilitating the upward price movement. Because the government operating budget tends to be inflexible in real terms, and because revenue comes largely from indirect taxes, the rise in prices generates fiscal deficits which are met by central bank borrowing. Similarly, the higher cost-price level also "forces" the banking system to provide additional private credit. While tight money could thus prevent the cost-price rise, with import and agricultural prices rising autonomously, a fall in industrial prices and wages would be required. Since both are sticky downward, a substantial drop in output and employment would be needed to force them down. Moreover, the relative rigidity of the government operating budget means that the alternative to central bank credit would be primarily a reduction in public investment. Since the low social boiling point in Latin American countries is rapidly approached when per capita output stagnates or falls and urban unemployment rises, efforts to maintain tight money are soon aborted, as has frequently been demonstrated in postwar Latin American experience.

Monetarists are thus stressing an irrelevancy when they point out that inflation cannot be sustained without a continued expansion of the money supply and can therefore be checked by halting the expansion. To do so for long without exacerbating social tensions is not possible unless per capita output and employment are expanding. Given the existing productive structure and class hostilities in Latin American countries, such a stabilization program could succeed only if external circumstances were favorable, as during a sustained export boom. Alternatively, tight money might be maintained by a strong dictatorship which is able to plug the outlets for the expression of social discontent.

The model as thus far outlined, however, merely states that the implementation of a stabilization program is devilishly difficult.[8] Still to be answered is the "monetarist" contention that the struc-

8. The "merely" is academic arrogance. For the hard-pressed Latin American politician, the adverse initial repercussions of such a program have generally sufficed to force its gradual abandonment.

tural rigidities and social tensions have been largely the result rather than the cause of the inflation.

"Structuralists," of course, argue the causal priority of the supply rigidities which generate chronic inflationary pressures and the monopoly pricing and social tensions which generalize these specific upward price movements. To buttress their case they refer to the pre-industrialization era in Latin America and to the conditions which have guided the subsequent industrialization effort.

Prior to 1930, when Latin American countries were "export economies" *par excellence,* inflationary trends were milder, it is pointed out, for the following reasons. World demand for Latin American mineral and agricultural exports had been expanding rapidly. Despite the organizational and technical backwardness of the *latifundios,* easily accessible virgin land facilitated the expansion of cultivation and pasture, so that the supply elasticity of agricultural output was relatively high. High death rates held down population growth, and most of the increase of the labor force could be absorbed by expanding agriculture. The "social question" was barely making its appearance in the post-World War I decade; trade unionism was weak, illiteracy retarded the growth of a demanding white collar and professional class, and political power rested safely with the agrarian and commercial aristocracy. Yet despite these favorable conditions, private domestic investment was flaccid and largely concentrated in agriculture, commerce and urban real estate. Mineral exports were mainly supplied by foreign-owned enterprises, while the major share of railroads and public utilities were foreign owned and operated. Low taxes retarded expenditure on public works and public services, although in the 1920's this expenditure rose considerably with the aid of large-scale foreign loans. In sum, Latin American countries entered their industrialization era burdened with a domestic capitalist class of limited investment horizons and weak propensities to accumulate, and a low and regressive tax structure which hampered public capital formation.

The crisis of the 1930's was more than an economic depression set off by a sharp drop in demand for Latin American exports and worsened by bootless attempts to service the heavy foreign debt. It was also in the more advanced Latin American countries a crisis of the political and social order. This crisis was resolved, however, by the end of the 1930's, by a somewhat shaky compromise. Grudgingly the "oligarchy" made room for a more pluralistic political system in which the demands of the white collar and professional classes and the urban workers could find expression. Strictures against unions were eased and social security and related welfare measures were introduced. The result was freer expression of wage demands and added pressures on a public budget whose revenues were still constrained by the entrenched system of low and regressive taxes.

A high rate of economic growth thus became a *sine qua non* for reconciling the competing income demands of the various social classes. The problem was compounded by two additional developments. One was the population explosion induced by DDT and other simple improvements in public health; a sharp drop in death rates has given Latin America in the past two decades the highest population growth rates in the world. The other was the exhaustion of the growth potential of the *latifundios* with their low yields per acre and per man. Further expansion now required either heavy investment to open up less accessible land or a substantial raising of yields through technical improvements and a shift to new products. Even had the transformation proceeded with reasonable rapidity it is unlikely that agriculture could have maintained its role as major employer of the recruits to the labor force, since many of the necessary innovations would have been labor saving. Nevertheless, a rapid rate of transformation would have at least meant cheap food for the cities and a growing rural market for urban products. Instead, the worst ensued. A rapid rate of agricultural modernization proved too much for the sluggish organizational structure of the *latifundios* and the weak investment propensities of the estate owners. Output expansion was slow, food prices pressed upward, and agriculture lost most of its ability to employ the growing population. The result was a heavy influx into the major cities well ahead of the growth of regular job opportunities, to be absorbed in personal services and the casual trades, both legal and illegal, and to be housed in rapidly growing shantytowns and crowded tenements. The influx intensified the clamor for regular employment and created demands on the government for low-cost housing, since private construction continued to concentrate on middle- and high-income housing.

Industrialization was enthusiastically selected as the chief means for achieving a viable rate of growth, for it promised better employment for the urban workers and white collar and professional classes, and reduced social tensions and relief from threats of agrarian reform to the propertied classes. But the conditions surrounding the industrialization effort gave substance to the "structuralist" model of inflation.

First, the slow growth of agricultural output made stable food prices incompatible with rising per capita income and rapid population growth.[9] Rising food prices affect with varying severity the real income of the urban classes, budget studies indicating that the proportion spent on food ranges from 50–60 per cent of disposable income for blue collar workers, 40 per cent for white collar workers, to progressively smaller percentages for higher income groups. Thus even with a stable aggregate price level and no compensating wage adjustments, a substantial part of each increment to real wages and salaries would be lost in higher food prices,[10] and there would be a chronic tendency for income distribution in the urban sector to shift adversely for the wage-salary classes. Understandably, wage and salary demands have been sensitive to rising food prices. To the extent that these demands have been acceded to by government legislation or private bargaining, industrial costs have risen and a food-wage-price spiral has set in, with prices rising by a multiple of the initial increase of food prices. In turn this has provoked governmental attempts to control food prices and exports, and to subsidize food imports.

The removal of these interferences with the market mechanism is one of the chief goals of the IMF-sponsored stabilization programs. But if the analysis is correct, the chronic food supply and demand imbalance would not be eliminated unless either the growth in per capita income is held to a rate compatible with the growth of the food suply or the wage-salary classes can be made to accept a slower growth of real wages than the real per capita in-

9. Assume the following plausible values: a 2.5 per cent annual growth in population, a 2 per cent annual increase in per capita income, and a 0.6 per cent income elasticity of demand for food. A 3.8 per cent growth in food supply would then be needed to preserve stable food prices. None of the industrializing Latin American countries with the exception of Mexico have been able to sustain such a rate of increase of domestic food output.

10. The loss would be the greater, the more price inelastic is the demand for food.

come growth of other social groups without the temporary solace of money wage-salary adjustments.

The chronic rise of import prices stems from another imbalance, the tendency for the Latin American demand for imports to outrun the demand for Latin American exports. This alleged aggregate relationship need not, of course, hold for each individual country, e.g., for Venezuela, which had the foresight to locate on a series of huge oil pools, or Mexico, which is conveniently situated to sell tourism to its high-income neighbor. Restricting ourselves, however, to aggregative relations between Latin America and its trading partners, the United States and industrial Europe, the argument runs as follows. The income elasticity of demand for Latin American exports, which consist overwhelmingly of raw materials and specialized foodstuffs, is less than unity. That is, the demand for these products rises less than the rise of real gross national product in the United States and other industrial regions. The reason is the well-documented fact that the income elasticity of demand for food is less than unity and the added fact that technological improvements — secondary recovery of metals, chemical substitutes, etc. — have tended to more than offset diminishing returns to natural resources, thus reducing the real cost of raw material inputs per unit of output. On the other hand, Latin American demand for the exports of its trading partners is greater than unity. This is particularly true of the demand for capital goods, since the indigenous capital goods industry is inadequately small.[11] It is also true, however, of consumer imports. For with the domestic service sector already grossly oversized for existing levels of per capita income due to the excess of underemployed urban labor, the marginal propensity to spend would be high for such items of convenience and status as consumer durables, nylons, wrist watches and cosmetics — were freedom to import these items maintained.

Thus, with no deliberate interference with the technological and behavioral forces determining these demand relationships, Latin American countries would be unable to maintain a rate of growth

11. The income elasticity of demand for mineral fuels — petroleum and coking coal — is also very high. Except for the handful of Latin American countries with ample domestic oil production, fuel imports have risen much more rapidly than real GNP.

of per capita income equal to that of the advanced countries, even were they to sustain equivalent savings-to-income ratios, without incurring repeated balance-of-payments crises and devaluations. Rising import prices would be a chronic source of inflationary pressure. Nor would foreign investment eliminate the exchange shortage, since under free market conditions it would be directed to the development of primary exports and guided closely by the demand for these exports. Given the social necessity of a high growth rate, the choice reduces itself to the means of meeting the chronic foreign exchange shortage: whether to incur repeated open devaluation or to slow its frequency by exchange and import controls. Both alternatives are inherently inflationary.[12]

The second alternative was generally chosen, in part because it could also be used to induce private industrial investment. Selective restriction of imports raised domestic prices and encouraged the production of local substitutes. Preferential exchange rates for the importation of raw materials and equipment were a supplementary stimulus. These methods, however, had many deficiencies. The authorities, pressed by competing demands for foreign exchange, curtailed "non-essential" consumer imports by import quotas and prohibitions rather than by high consumption taxes. They thereby biased private investment toward the production of these non-essentials. Since many of the new industries were largely dependent on imported materials and fuels, industrial production became increasingly vulnerable to cutbacks in the capacity to import. There was, in addition, a general tendency to overvalue export exchange rates and thus somewhat to discourage exports.[13] On the other hand, most of the influx of foreign manufacturing investment in the past two decades was induced by import restrictions, and would probably not have come in, given the higher Latin American production costs, if freedom to

12. This is the essence of the "Prebisch thesis," advanced by Dr. Raúl Prebisch, the influential director of the United Nations Economic Commission for Latin America. The thesis is a basic tenet not only in the writings of the Commission but also in popular discussions of Latin America's economic problems.

13. This need not have been so in principle. In practice, since the authorities wished to give preferential rates to certain classes of imports while preserving some exchange rate profits for the treasury, the downward adjustment of export rates tended to lag behind the rise in domestic costs.

import finished manufactures had been maintained. On balance, however, many of the "structuralists" concede that exchange controls had become excessively cumbersome and a prime source of corruption by the 1950's, and have welcomed the simplifications introduced under the stabilization programs.[14] What they deny is that these simplifications would resolve the underlying foreign exchange problem and its inflationary consequences.

Despite optimistic projections, relative industrial prices did not fall much after the new industries had gained a foothold. Domestic markets were small; once imports had been replaced, further growth depended mainly on the growth of income and its distribution. But though income rose, agricultural stagnation and the highly unequal distribution of urban income retarded the formation of mass markets. A pronounced tendency toward single-firm or oligopolistic industries and undersized plants permeated the Latin American industrial structure. In addition, low tax revenues, additionally curbed by tax concessions to encourage the industrial investment, and the competing "social demands" on the budget retarded public investment. Thus transport bottlenecks, power shortages and an inadequate growth of industrial and technical educational facilities held back improvements in industrial efficiency. The monopoloid market structures, however, enabled increases in industrial costs to be passed on readily in higher prices. "Structuralists" will generally concede that increased import competition and tighter credit would force greater efficiency from the existing industrial structure.[15] What they contend, however, is that if these devices are applied forcefully they may topple the high-cost industrial structure — a dubious accomplishment — without setting into motion new growth forces sufficient to restore a high rate of economic growth.

By the mid-1950's industrial growth had begun to slacken. Consumer imports, other than foodstuffs, had been so compressed that opportunities for further import substitution at the consumer level had dwindled. Import substitution at the capital goods level was restrained by the shortage of government investment funds

14. This is, for example, the consensus among Chilean "structuralists," according to Grunwald. (See his paper.)

15. It is interesting to note that under the Chilean and Argentine stabilization efforts, industrial employment has fallen while industrial output has more or less held to a constant level.

and the reluctance of private capital to risk funds in large-scale capital-intensive ventures. Externally, export prices weakened and terms of trade fell, cutting tax revenues from the export sector and intensifying the foreign exchange problem. Preferential exchange rates for industry were curbed, successive devaluations took place and inflation accelerated. An economic and social crisis threatened again.

Two things should be clear from this summary of the "structuralist" position. First, the "structuralists" do not regard inflation as a viable long-run solution to Latin America's growth problems. Rather it is viewed as a manifestation of a deformed economy. Second, they concede that an IMF-type stabilization program may reduce some of the deformities in the economy — the secondary malfunctions. But what the programs do not remedy are more basic imbalances which retard economic growth. They thus introduce a degree of greater efficiency at the cost of reduced employment and stagnating output, a socially untenable solution.

To which countries does the "structuralist" model apply? Probably its relevance to Chile can be most easily defended; for other countries various qualifications are necessary. For example, there has been only a small acceleration of population growth in Argentina in the past two decades. And it is questionable, moreover, whether the poor post-war performance of Argentine agriculture can be attributed mainly to the inefficiency of the *latifundios*. Similarly, the sheer size of Brazil's population seems, despite the low per capita income, to have given that country greater scope for shifting industrialization to capital goods. The relative growth of the urban sector, and hence the attendant social problems, has not been as great in Peru and Colombia as in Brazil or Chile. Whether these and perhaps other qualifications seriously restrict the validity of the model cannot, however, be ascertained without more careful research than has thus far been undertaken.

On the other hand, empirical support for the "monetarist" position is rather sparse. There is simply a paucity of rapidly growing non-inflationary economies extant in Latin America today. Venezuela with its prolonged oil boom is clearly a special case, turned somewhat sour, moreover, since 1958 when the boom slackened and domestic prices began rising. Mexico, although its "price stability" encompasses an annual rate of inflation of 7.5 per cent for 1953–59,[16] perhaps offers support, *faute de mieux*, for the "monetarist" position. But with its prior agrarian reform and unique (for Latin America) social and political cohesiveness deriving from the Revolution, Mexico can also buttress the "structuralist" case for agrarian reform as a prerequisite for balanced growth and relative stability. In the countries attempting the IMF cure, there has been, despite supporting foreign loans, neither a marked resurgence of economic growth nor social pacification. In Chile, where the cure has been under way since the fall of 1955, per capita income has remained more or less stagnant and social tensions high. The Argentine cure has been of shorter duration, but the consequences have thus far been broadly similar.

What are the "structuralist" alternatives? While it is clear that they would include economic and social reforms to give greater balance and flexibility to the productive structure and a deeper sense of social cohesion, the specifics vary and the details are distressingly vague. It is never clearly indicated, for example, whether or not the reforms during their gestation period would require an inflationary monetary and fiscal policy. This vagueness is, as suggested earlier, due to the fact that the "structuralists" are critics without as yet the power and responsibility to make and implement policy. They can thus voice desirable aspirations without demonstrating that they are mutually consistent. A detailed listing of proposed reforms would thus be tedious, probably incomplete, and not very illuminating as regards inflation.

A useful division, however, is between "structuralists" who would work within the social establishment to reform it and those to whom revolutionary surgery – a socialist revolution – is essential. Major revolutions are rarely compatible with price level stability, so that implicitly the latter group would put off the goal of price stability until the institutional groundwork has been drastically relaid.

For the first group reconciliation with the "monetarists" is more immediately possible – in theory. For example, within the framework of a tight money policy, fiscal instruments could effect various structural reforms: differentially heavy consumption taxes could check the penchant of private investment for the production

16. Based on the cost-of-living index. For 1939–52 the annual rate of increase was 12.2 per cent.

of luxuries; heavier land taxes, whose impact would be relatively more severe the more underutilized and inefficient the *latifundio*, could accelerate agrarian reorganization. By imparting a sense of equality of sacrifice badly lacking in the current stabilization programs, such taxation might also modify wage-salary demands. And the augmented public investment made possible could hasten the removal of transport and power bottlenecks, facilitate the growth of a capital goods industry and aid agricultural development.

The main difficulty lies not, however, in devising academic solutions which could reconcile stability with economic growth, but in achieving the social consensus which would permit such solutions to be implemented. Would the fiscal program suggested above ever be acceptable to the Latin American propertied classes? Would it, with its paucity of demagoguery, even appeal to the masses? Is it at all likely that the tax collector could become the agent for pacifying the battling social classes? And between Bourbonism on the Right and demagoguery on the Left is it likely that alternative solutions would fare much better? The social attitudes suggested by these questions rather than the intractability of the structural imbalances are perhaps the chief obstacles to a joint "monetarist"–"structuralist" resolution of the inflation problem.

THE "STRUCTURALIST" SCHOOL ON PRICE STABILIZATION AND ECONOMIC DEVELOPMENT: THE CHILEAN CASE

by JOSEPH GRUNWALD

FOR at least the last five years an acrimonious public debate has been carried on in Latin America between the so-called "monetarist" and "structuralist" schools in regard to the nature of inflation. This may be considered a corollary of the now overworked "demand-pull" versus "cost-push" discussion in the United States of the last few years, although the "structuralist" and the "cost-push" arguments seem to have little in common. However, both the "structuralists" of Latin America and the adherents to the "cost-push" school in the United States challenge orthodox thinking on the inflation problem.[1]

The underlying policy question in both debates is whether monetary stabilization policies are compatible with economic growth. There is hardly any questioning of the ability of monetary policies to achieve price stability, but the discussion runs in terms

1. Just as the "cost-push" discussion has not been confined to the United States but applies also to other highly industrialized countries (particularly England), so the "structuralist" arguments have been articulated in less developed areas outside of Latin America.

Joseph Grunwald is Director of the Institute of Economic Research of the University of Chile, Santiago. *The author is indebted to the following "structuralists," "monetarists" and innocent bystanders who have read an early draft of this paper and have made helpful comments: Thomas Balogh, Robert T. Brown, Tom Davis, Luis Escobar, Arnold Harberger, Carlos Massad, Aníbal Pinto and John Strasma.*

of whether such stability is achieved only through underutilization of resources with the social costs far greater than those of the inflation it strives to cure.[2] There is naturally a vast difference in degree of emphasis between the two debates simply because the objective of economic development is more in the forefront in Latin America than in the United States.

It is the purpose of this paper to examine the "structuralist" school of thought on inflation in Latin America with special reference to the Chilean case. The principal objective is to present these ideas in a neutral fashion. While this report contains clarifying and critical comments, an analytic critique of "structuralist" thought is outside its scope.

Although the view of the need for some inflation for the purposes of economic development is not without its adherents in Latin America, the "structuralist" school is not concerned with the problem of stability *or* economic development but rather with the problem of how to make stability compatible with economic development.[3]

The essence of the "structuralist" argument is that price stability can be attained only through economic growth. The basic forces of inflation are structural in nature. Financial factors might be important, but only as forces propagating inflation and not originating it. It is admitted that monetary policy can be easily managed and has relatively quick effects, but it attacks only symptoms and therefore cannot cure.

On the other hand the idea is rejected of putting the monetary house in order *first,* before policies directly related to economic development can be introduced. "Structuralists" will hardly deny that inflation can go on for very long without monetary expansion. But this they consider irrelevant. They are concerned with the underlying forces which bring such pressure on the monetary

2. Of course the arguments never deal with runaway inflation. However, the concept of what is a "severe" and what a "mild" inflation varies sharply between the United States and Latin America. Thus in the United States a "mild" inflation might be up to 3 or 5 per cent per year, while in Chile, for instance, it might extend to 10 or 12 per cent per year (see the discussion on Chilean inflation history further on).

3. There is no doubt, however, that, when faced with these alternatives, economic development would have definite priority. See Celso Furtado, "Da objetividade do economista," Instituto de Ciências Económicas, Políticas e Sociais de Minas Gerais, Belo Horizonte, Brazil, 1959.

authorities as to make expansion of the money supply nearly inevitable. Even when monetary policy has successfully diminished total demand, the argument goes, the underlying inflationary pressures will persist and may even be intensified. In the best of cases stability will be attained at the cost of economic growth.

Argentina, Brazil, Chile and Mexico are the countries in which the discussion has been most articulate, but the development problems vary widely among the four countries. The Chilean case will be discussed here summarily, not only because of the writer's familiarity with it, but also because, in his view, the debate in that country has greater relevance than elsewhere in Latin America.

INFLATION IN CHILE[5]

Recent Economic Growth

Fragmentary and incomplete data suggest that per capita gross national product has increased at an average annual rate of about one per cent since the beginning of the century.[4] Since 1940, the first year for which fairly reliable national income statistics are available, gross national product has increased by an average of 5 per cent annually up to 1953 but only by about one per cent

4. Tom Davis and Marto Ballesteros, *The Growth of Output in Basic Sectors of the Chilean Economy*, 1908–1957, Santiago, 1959 (mimeo.).

5. For general background material on the Chilean economy, see:

Instituto de Economía, *Desarrollo económico de Chile, 1940–1956,* Editorial Universitaria, S.A., Santiago, 1956.

Corporación de Fomento de la Producción, *Cuentas nacionales de Chile, 1940–1957,* Editorial del Pacífico, S.A., Santiago, 1957.

Also:

Ahumada, Jorge, *En vez de la miseria,* Edit. del Pacífico, 1958.

Ellsworth, Paul T., *Chile, an Economy in Transition,* The Macmillan Company, New York, 1945.

Grunwald, Joseph, *Outlook for Chile's Foreign Trade and Economic Growth, 1959–1965,* Instituto de Economía, Santiago, 1958.

Pinto S.-C., Aníbal, *Chile, un caso de desarrollo frustrado,* Editorial Universitaria, S.A., Santiago, 1959.

For discussion of inflation and economic growth see:

Deaver, John, *La inflación chilena como un impuesto,* Universidad Católica de Chile, Santiago, 1957.

Economic Commission for Latin America, U. N., "Algunos Aspectos Inflacionarios en Chile," *Boletín Económico de América Latina,* Jan. 1956.

Escobar, Luis, "Desocupación con inflación – El caso chileno," *Panorama Económico,* Santiago, No. 205, August 1959.

Felix, David, *Desequilibrios estructurales y crecimiento industrial – El*

annually between 1953 and 1959. Because population has been increasing at the rate of 2.5 per cent per annum in recent years[6] this means that 1959 per capita income was below the 1953 level.

Between 1953 and 1959 per capita consumption levels were maintained only at the expense of investment. Since 1940, gross investment rarely has exceeded 12 per cent of gross national product in Chile, but in the last three years it even has fallen below 10 per cent. While this permitted average consumption per person to hold steady in the face of a rapidly increasing population and slowly growing GNP, it is probable that consumption of lower income groups has fallen because of the adverse effects of inflation on the distribution of income.[7]

The structure of the economy has changed considerably in the last two decades. Income generated in agriculture declined from 20 to 15 per cent of total national income since 1940, while the manufacturing industry share increased from 12 to about 20 per cent of the total. About 28 per cent of the labor force is now employed in agriculture as compared with 36 per cent in 1940. Manufacturing industry now employs about one fifth of the labor force as compared with 16 per cent in 1940. There also has been an increase in the proportion of the working population in commerce and services, whose relative contribution to national income has remained unchanged. On the other hand, employment in mining has decreased as productivity has risen.

---

caso chileno, Instituto de Economía, Santiago, 1958.

Felix, David, "Structural Imbalances, Social Conflict, and Inflation," *Economic Development and Cultural Change,* Chicago, Vol. VIII, No. 2, Jan. 1960.

Kaldor, Nicholas, "Problemas económicos de Chile," *El Trimestre Económico,* Mexico City, No. 102, April–June 1959, pp. 170–221.

Klein & Saks Mission, *El programa de estabilización de la economía chilena y el trabajo de la Misión Klein & Saks,* Edit. Universitaria, Santiago, 1958.

Pinto S.-C., Aníbal, *Ni estabilidad ni desarrollo – La política del Fondo Monetario Internacional,* Santiago, 1960.

Sunkel, Osvaldo, "La inflación chilena – Un enfoque heterodoxo," *El Trimestre Económico,* Mexico City, No. 100, Oct.–Dec. 1958.

See also the pertinent chapters in the *Economic Surveys of Latin America,* of ECLA, for 1954, 1957 and 1958.

6. Chile's National Statistics Service estimates the country's population at 7¼ million at the end of 1959.

7. The official cost-of-living adjustments of manual workers' wages since 1953 have not kept up with the index of consumer prices.

In this over-all picture the outstanding impression is a relatively slow growth of agricultural production, which has barely been able to keep up with the population increase. Chile not only was nearly self-sufficient in agriculture some twenty years ago, but in some products even had an export surplus. Yet now the country is spending close to one fifth of its import budget on imports of foodstuffs.[8]

Inflation History

There is some evidence that Chile's price inflation started as far back as the late 1870's. Since the beginning of the official consumer price index in 1928, there have been only about four years, but not consecutive ones, during which it may be said that relative price stability existed.

Chile's very severe depression of the 1930's and the influence of the war years of the forties brought a very erratic pattern of price movements during those two decades. On the average, the yearly price increase was roughly 10 per cent during the thirties and 20 per cent during the forties. The inflation rate increased somewhat during the first years of the fifties, but in the middle of 1953 a price explosion took place which brought the yearly inflation rate to over 80 per cent by 1955. With the 1956 anti-inflation program the inflation rate dropped to 38 per cent in 1956 and 17 per cent in 1957. Price increases were higher in 1958 and 1959, reaching about 35 per cent annually, but since the end of 1959 a relative stability has been attained.

Inflation became a way of life and was institutionalized into the legal and socio-economic structure of the country, each sector of the economy constructing its own defense apparatus.

The wage and salary sectors achieved the right to legal wage readjustments in some relation to the cost-of-living index. These income adjustments applied not only to wages and salaries but also to pensions, retirement and other social security incomes. The

8. Data of the University of Chile's Institute of Economic Research indicate that imports of foodstuffs amounted to 6 per cent of total import value in 1940, compared to an average of 19 per cent for the years 1954–59. However, it must be pointed out that a large part of this increase is accounted for by "non-competitive" imports, such as tea, coffee, sugar, etc.

other mechanism for the salaried classes was price control and subsidized imports of certain basic consumer items.[9]

The self-employed and profit-earning groups defended themselves first through anticipating the inflation by increasing their prices even before the annual wage adjustments came around, and following this up by further price increases after the wage adjustments were given. Second, the credit mechanism also served as an inflation defense for the more substantial businesses. Increases in costs due to wage adjustments and price increases of raw materials were readily absorbed through relatively easy access to credit for the privileged groups, while for others credit was sharply rationed or unavailable.

The government sector defended itself against inflation through the printing press. It is clear that deficit spending became unavoidable as government revenues were based upon the previous period's assessments compared to current pricing for government expenditures.[10]

Nearly all of the sectors of the community hedged through the building up of inventories. This applied also to consumer groups, who bought consumer goods for storage rather than for use.

It is not surprising that this inflation spirit developed a finesse and cleverness in handling the pressures of price increases in all sectors. Although most of the defense mechanisms employed were in themselves quite inflationary, there is little doubt that they brought a certain self-confidence to the community which helped to stave off panic.[11]

9. While even under price control maximum prices increase in a continuing inflation, at a given moment the maximum price is below the level of what an uncontrolled price would be.

10. It is curious to note that according to Chilean law, government deficits are illegal. The government got around this provision by having Congress pass a balanced budget at the beginning of the fiscal year and then enacting special expenditure laws to meet the additional costs.

11. The curious aspect of Chile's inflation history of close to a century is that the country never experienced runaway inflation. One would think that, once a country reaches such high rates of price increases as Chile did, hyperinflation would follow almost automatically. There is no satisfactory answer to this. The fact is that not enough money was printed for hyperinflation to develop. But if the forces that made the authorities "print money" were so strong as to maintain a 20 or more per cent yearly inflation for many years, what stopped those forces from compelling a snowballing monetary expansion? Probably the social pressures were not strong enough, and perhaps

Stabilization Efforts

The country nevertheless was not happy to live with continuous price increases. Almost every year attempts were made to control inflation. Most of these stabilization efforts consisted of some sort of monetary controls and some of them were relatively successful for a few months at a time until they broke down when pressures for credit became irresistible. Credit restriction, which was the principal tool of anti-inflation policy,[12] could not be maintained as production costs increased by an enormous leap each time the yearly wage and salary cost-of-living adjustments came around.[13] Such massive cost increases could not be absorbed by the companies out of their working capital. These recurrent wage adjustments together with other periodic surges of demands for credit during the wheat harvest and at tax payment dates caused a practically seasonal breakdown of stabilization policy.

It is understandable, therefore, that these stabilization efforts did not change the expectations of the business and consumer community but, on the contrary, each failure reinforced the inflation spirit of the nation. Finance and economics ministers came and went as they disagreed with the Executive or saw their efforts frustrated by vested interests or failed because of incompetence. This turnover of ministers who were given the responsibility of bringing stability to the economy naturally fortified the belief that inflation was here to stay.

The exceptional impetus that price increases reached in 1954 and 1955 did alarm public opinion and made the time ripe for bringing to the country a foreign mission to act as a political catalyst in this problem. The recommendations of the Klein-Saks mission, a United States private consulting firm which was em-

public confidence was greater than is generally thought. But if among the factors of hyperinflation is public panic, then the defense mechanisms which the Chilean community has built up over the years have helped to avoid it – no matter how inflationary these mechanisms may be in themselves.

12. Of course not all "anti-inflation" attempts were based on credit restrictions exclusively but also on other measures such as the frustrated 1953 attempt to eliminate the repressed inflation through the lifting of price controls.

13. Not all wage and salary adjustments came at the same time, but there is no question that substantial "bunching" did take place.

ployed in the second half of 1955,[14] to everybody's great surprise, won relatively wide political support. Thus, in the beginning of 1956 the government was able to institute a rather severe anti-inflation program. Here it must be noted that this program consisted of measures which had been recommended by some Chilean economists for a long time but who were ineffectual within a political atmosphere of mutual suspicion. Each economist was identified with a political party or opinion and doubt was cast on his intellectual integrity by the opposing political opinion.

In 1956 Parliament agreed to limit wage adjustments to one-half of the previous twelve-and-a-half-month increase in the cost-of-living index (45 per cent adjustment in wages and salaries in the face of an over 90 per cent increase in the cost of living). Credit restraints were also instituted and, what was even more important, the fantastic multiplicity of foreign exchange rates and import controls was radically reduced so that the whole foreign trade apparatus was made more efficient.

The realization that such measures were politically feasible constituted the first significant shock to the inflation spirit of the country. This does not mean that businessmen's and consumers' expectations were completely reversed, but there is no question that the inflation expectations were shaken, and this was enough to change purchasing habits somewhat. The tendency to buy for storage was reduced. The loss of purchasing power through the wage restraint also dampened buying activity. Producers found themselves squeezed between loss of sales and tighter money.

The first victim, as might be expected, was the construction industry, which in 1956 dropped to one-half of the feverish activity reached during 1955, a peak year. Inefficient industries became exposed as preferential exchange rates were eliminated and the umbrella of an inflation-stimulated demand was partially withdrawn. They could not make the cost-cutting adjustment to maintain production, and many firms found themselves either bankrupt or operating far below capacity.[15] Significant unemployment ensued. The Institute of Economic Research of the Univer-

14. One of the important factors in hiring the Klein-Saks mission was its apparent success in helping Peru stop its inflation in the early fifties.

15. Chile's Development Corporation estimated, on the basis of a broad survey, that manufacturing industry operated at an average of 47 per cent of capacity in 1957.

sity of Chile, which has conducted unemployment surveys since 1956 in the urban centers of the nation, measured unemployment at 7 per cent of the labor force at the end of 1956, a level from which Chile has not recovered.[16]

The Klein-Saks policies brought some results on the stabilization front. Price increases in 1956 declined to 38 per cent, and to 17 per cent in 1957 as already mentioned. While these figures represent significant improvements considering the previous experience, they could not be called an unqualified success, particularly when considering the sacrifice of the salaried classes in respect to their purchasing power, unemployment and a general slowdown in productive activity. In any case the positive results of breaking the inflation were short-lived. The rate of price increases rose again in 1958 to 35 per cent and continued at this high level through the first year of the new government administration in 1959.[17]

The failure of the Klein-Saks mission in the long run was due to several factors. First of all the political problem again came to the fore with the impossibility of getting the whole of the mission's program accepted by the Executive or by Congress. The politically difficult aspects of the program, such as a tax reform, budget policy, and others, were either ignored or postponed. It was just the "structuralist" aspects of the program which the mission was not able to "sell" to the Chilean government.[18]

The sharp drop in the copper price in 1957 contributed to the

16. Unemployment might have existed already before 1956. The census of 1952 indicated a 5 per cent unemployment in the Greater Santiago area. The rate was 7 per cent of the labor force in Greater Santiago at the end of 1960. (See the period survey reports on "Ocupación y desocupación," Instituto de Economía, Universidad de Chile, Santiago.)

17. The Klein-Saks mission operated during the administration of President Ibáñez from August 1955 to July 1958. Its contract was terminated before the presidential elections of September, when Alessandri was elected.

18. Nevertheless, the mission was blamed for the failure as if the recommendations which were accepted constituted its whole program. Even many of those persons who were sympathetic to the mission expected this foreign entity to act like a local finance minister: it should have resigned if essential points in its recommendations for the stabilization effort were not accepted. These people felt that the Executive would not have let the mission resign and would have yielded to the demand to include all important parts of the program in government policy. The mission itself rationalized its staying on by claiming that in this manner it could at least give some guidance and that through its presence it prevented the government from a possible return to the road of aimless policy wanderings.

failure of the stabilization program. While the price of copper rose sharply during the first half of 1956, thus undoubtedly aiding the government's anti-inflation effort, the drop that followed was considerably greater than the previous gain. As a consequence a substantial government deficit emerged and the expectations of the business community were adversely affected.

The stagnation in economic activity and unemployment brought pressure to ease credit and wage restraints.[19] Thus, in 1958, and to some extent already in 1957, wage readjustments corresponded to practically the full amount of the consumer price increase. A significant part of the business community evaded the wage restraints imposed by the government, at least as far as their white collar workers were concerned, and gave salary increases in excess of the percentage indicated by the law.

A last point must not be overlooked. The composition of the board of directors of Chile's Central Bank largely explains the difficulty that existed of enforcing effective credit restraints. The board was dominated by private banking interests, which often neglected the public interest in favor of their own and that of privileged clients.

The administration of President Alessandri, which came to power at the end of 1958, instituted its own anti-inflation program. This resembled quite closely the Klein-Saks policy in its basic features but was not identified as such by the government. Credit restraints were tightened, finally reaching the point of eliminating completely the rediscount privilege of the private banks at Chile's Central Bank.[20] For obvious political considerations, wage restraints were not imposed during the first year of the new administration. The legal wage adjustments for both 1958 and 1959 for some sectors were set at a higher percentage than the previous year's cost-of-living increase.[21]

19. A strong negative factor in this picture was the lack of adequate foreign financial support. Although the government's stabilization efforts were unanimously applauded abroad, sufficient resources could not be obtained from the International Monetary Fund, and the International Bank for Reconstruction and Development maintained itself completely aloof from Chile's need.

20. Marginal reserve requirements were also raised sharply on peso and dollar deposits.

21. The new government attempted to level wage differentials giving higher wage adjustments to the lowest-paid workers.

The new stabilization policy has relied heavily on the building up of business and public confidence in the government and the economy. A unitary free rate of exchange was established and, for the first time in many years, it has been possible to maintain it at a constant level for an extended period.[22] The local banks were permitted to accept dollar deposits at a substantial rate of interest (8 per cent annually) and the government issued dollar notes and bonds of high yield. These measures were designed to repatriate some of the private capital which went abroad during the peak inflation period. On the other hand, in this new regime the banking system was committed to extend dollar loans. These, to some extent, were used as money substitutes and thus acted to increase the money supply of the economy. In this manner new inflationary pressures were generated. In addition, the extremely attractive yields of the dollar deposits and bonds discouraged funds from going into productive investments,[23] if it is considered that many uses made by banks of their dollar deposits and by the government of proceeds of bond issues were relatively sterile.[24]

Another essential aspect and a completely new one in the recent stabilization effort has been "moral suasion." The government, through a special committee, has undertaken a vigorous consumer education campaign in an attempt to create resistance on the part of the consumer to price increases.[25]

22. The rate of exchange has remained at 1,050 Chilean pesos to the United States dollar since January 1959.

23. Chile's new import regulations required advance deposits of varying magnitudes before imports could be effected. These deposits could be made in dollar bonds issued by the government. Thus it was possible to buy a government dollar bond at about 8 per cent annual interest and lend it out to a bank or an importer in order to satisfy his import deposit requirements. For this loan the bondholder could obtain as high as 3 per cent per month so that the effective interest return to the bondholder reached about 45 per cent a year. Under more recent regulations such high yields are no longer possible.

24. Substantial amounts of the dollar loans extended by the banks were for the purpose of luxury imports.

25. In addition to newspaper and radio campaigns, such methods have been employed as loudspeakers from low-flying planes and a campaign to encourage consumers to denounce stores that increase prices, although, except for some "essentials," there is no legal restraint on price increases. Newspapers friendly to the government have given publicity to the denouncements on the one hand, and on the other have published lists of stores that have pledged to join the campaign of maintaining prices.

Attempts were made to eliminate most of the factors repressing inflation, so that now very few price controls remain. Business confidence was bolstered by the successful contraction of foreign loans and these loans also helped in balancing the budget.

While inflation continued at full speed during the first year of the new administration, when the consumer price index rose by about 35 per cent, since the end of 1959 an unaccustomed price stability has taken hold. The cost-of-living index between November 1959 and June 1960 remained stationary for all practical purposes. There is no question that the "moral suasion" campaign, in spite of all ridicule, made itself felt effectively, but the fact that the government was able to hold off the passing of any legal wage readjustment in the beginning of 1960 helped considerably.[26] Also, the fact that it was possible to maintain a close rein on credit expansion contributed to the attainment of stability. Chile's recent earthquake disaster on the one hand has helped to create for the moment a spirit of national solidarity which has prevented the demands for the enactment of legal wage readjustments from becoming irresistible, but on the other hand will pose a tremendous challenge to the government's stabilization effort as the reconstruction program gets under way.

Almost simultaneously with the halting of the price increases at the end of 1959, the economy lost the impetus which it had attained during the first half of 1959.[27] By the middle of 1960 the economy could be described again as being in a state of semi-stagnation, as it has been most of the time since the mid-1950's. While the seismic catastrophes of May 1960 undoubtedly had some effects on economic activities, these effects were relatively small and, in any case, the slackening of production began to make itself felt several months before.

26. In effect, wages and salaries were left to individual and collective bargaining, but the Alessandri government has attempted to keep increases to 10 per cent through public pronouncements that any rate higher than that would be completely inflationary. In the first half of 1960 the average wage increase obtained through collective bargaining was about 17 per cent (as compared to the 10 per cent limit asked for by the President and the 35 per cent increase in the cost of living of the previous year). However, large sectors of the economy had not yet renegotiated their wage contracts by then. Only at the end of 1960 a general wage adjustment of 15 per cent was legislated.

27. This is not necessarily a correlation but a historical fact (or accident).

It is interesting to reflect here for a moment on the complexities of policy-making. Without examining the reasons for the recent loss of momentum of the Chilean economy, an important factor seems to have been the monetary restraint of the stabilization policy. Yet, by mid-1960 the banking system was liquid and it looked as if, of all things, bank loans might go begging. By the "monetarists" this was interpreted as a victory for the stabilization policy; by the "structuralists" it was seen as a demonstration of weak demand and of the declining or "lazy" economy in general. The fact of the matter is that it still costs the borrower over 25 per cent per annum for a bona fide bank loan in the face of almost complete price stability. Only a few months before, when the rate of inflation was 35 per cent per year, this meant a negative real rate of interest and anyone lucky enough to have access to bank loans could make speculative profits. But even after half a year of a constant price level, the bank interest rates hardly budged, and it is clear that 25 per cent per year in real terms is an impossible cost burden to carry for most enterprises. The downward stickiness of the interest rate came as a surprise[28] and was difficult to explain (except in terms of monopolistic banking practices, of which there is some evidence in Chile).

There were indications that the demand for bank loans was relatively elastic and that lower interest rates would stimulate credit expansion and with it business activity. The authorities, hoping for the effects of the free play of the market, had been hesitant to force the rate down either by decree or through some artifact. By the time they were ready to intervene and might have succeeded in lowering interest, the impact of the reconstruction program of the country's devastated regions started to make itself felt on the price level. A possible return of inflation would not be the propitious moment at which to lower the cost of borrowing, and so the opportunity for stimulating certain business activities by this means might be lost.

This episode merely goes to show that even monetary tools, which are considered to be among the more flexible policy mechanisms, are sufficiently complex and delicate to require for their

28. For many years, Chilean authorities have imposed a ceiling on the rates of interest banks may charge but, of course, there has never been a lower limit.

successful operation managers not only wise but also of great skill, sensitivity and quick decisions.

THE "STRUCTURALIST" SCHOOL[29]

It is not surprising that the long history of fiascos in the stabilization policies led to a deep division in the thinking on approaches to the country's economic problems. The growing young intellectual community became impatient with the lack of dynamism which had characterized the Chilean economy during recent years and which was aggravated by the policies of the stabilization program. The inability of these policies to attain price stability, of course, sharpened the dissent.

Traditional monetary policies were challenged already in the 1940's[30] but the issues on how to fight inflation did not become seriously defined until the 1950's and particularly after the advent of the Klein-Saks mission in Chile. The greater role of the International Monetary Fund in the lending policies of the international agencies and of the United States government from 1957 onward has brought the debate to the fore in other Latin American countries also.[31] There is no question but that those who

29. Among the best-argued expositions of the "structuralist" viewpoint, particularly as far as Chile is concerned, are "La inflación chilena – Un enfoque heterodoxo," by Osvaldo Sunkel, in *El Trimestre Económico,* and *Ni estabilidad ni desarrollo – La política del Fondo Monetario Internacional,* by Aníbal Pinto, both cited in note 5. See also Jorge Ahumada, *op. cit.,* and Luis Escobar, *op. cit.*

30. The often-time minister of finance Guillermo del Pedregal (1941–42, 1942–43 and 1953) was one of the first and also one of the most consistent detractors of orthodox monetary policy in favor of all-out orientation toward accelerating development.

One of Chile's top economists, Flavián Levine, also was one of the early critics of standard monetary policy as the exclusive anti-inflationary instrument. He cannot be considered, however, a precursor of the "structuralist" school because he emphasized automatic wage adjustments in excess of productivity growth as a basic factor underlying inflation. He is thus very close to the cost inflation school in the United States and England. See his *Cuentas nacionales 1954* published by the Institute of Economic Research of the University of Chile in 1954, articles in *Panorama Económico* and various memoranda between 1951 and 1955.

31. The International Monetary Fund is the chief exponent of traditional monetary policy in Latin America and elsewhere and a borrowing country must conform to certain IMF guidelines to be eligible for loans not only

doubt the efficacy of orthodox methods in fighting inflation have become an ever increasing group.

In all fairness, it must be stated that the dividing line between "monetarists" and "structuralists" is perhaps not as sharp as drawn here.[32] Some "structuralists" have exaggerated their differences with the "monetarists" for political or other reasons. It is obvious that the "monetarists" would agree with much of what the "structuralists" say and vice versa. If one examines the complete program of the Klein-Saks mission,[33] which came under such strong fire by the "structuralists," one will probably find one of the most "structural" programs that was ever proposed in Chile on a practical level. It was the International Monetary Fund which helped draw the lines of battle.

A. *The "Basic" Factors*

The challenge to the purely monetary approach was based on the belief that monetary policies attack only the symptoms of the sickness but provide no cure for it. Basic structural factors are seen as underlying the inflation and are distinguished sharply from circumstantial, cumulative or propagation factors. The "basic" factors are the causal forces of inflation. The propagation factors might also be important once an inflation is under way, but gearing policy only toward them, according to this view, will not eliminate inflationary pressures because the fundamental maladjustments will persist.

The "basic" or structural factors underlying inflation essentially are connected with the alleged inelasticity of supply and with the rigidity in the public financial apparatus. In other words, the

---

from the IMF but often also from other international and United States government agencies.

32. On this point see the writings of Felipe Herrera Lane, former Minister of Finance and General Manager of the Central Bank of Chile and now President of the Inter-American Development Bank: *¿Desarrollo económico o estabilidad monetaria?* Editorial Jurídica de Chile, Santiago, 1958; "Bases de la política económica del gobierno," *Panorama Económico,* Santiago, No. 82, July 31, 1953, pp. 449 *et seq.;* "La inflación chilena y la política fiscal," *Panorama Económico,* No. 117, March 4, 1955, pp. 80 *et seq.;* "Política económica y política monetaria," *Panorama Económico,* No. 180, Nov. 22, 1957, pp. 751 *et seq.*

33. See the Klein-Saks mission report, cited in note 5.

structural factors are closely related to the state of underdevelopment of the economy.

"Inelastic" Supply

A great many things go into the concept of "inelastic" supply.[34] This means roughly that the supply of goods and services does not expand and its composition does not adjust sufficiently fast to meet not only a rising demand but also a change in the pattern of demand without serious price pressures. Rigidity is particularly pronounced in the infrastructure of the economy, which in turn induces a lack of flexibility in production, particularly in agriculture where flexibility is low anyway because of the existing institutional arrangements. Obviously, an integral part of this picture is an inefficient labor and capital market or, to put it in other words, a low mobility of resources.

The inelasticity of the capacity to import or its sharp fluctuations in the short run are a chapter of the same story and so is the low saving rate with the accompanying low capital formation. Another factor is a monopolistic development in industry and in the distribution system, fostered principally by the small size of the domestic market. And one must not forget the personal income distribution, which, because of its high degree of inequality in lesser developed areas, plays an important role in this concept of "inelasticity" according to the "structuralists."

1. *Agriculture.* One explanation runs in the following terms: the increase in urbanization which accompanies economic growth signifies that an increasing share of the population depends upon commercially distributed agricultural products. Many of the people who are now in the city obtained a large part of their food requirements directly from the farm on which they worked before they migrated. This additional demand for commercial food products plus the change in the composition of demand due to urbanization plus the demand generated by the rapidly increasing population, can only be satisfied if the agricultural production system is sufficiently elastic to respond rapidly to the demand increases.

34. The "structuralists" seldom specify which concept of elasticity is meant. Sometimes price and often income elasticity are used under the general heading "elasticity."

This, however, is not the case for various reasons of which backward institutional arrangements are the most important.

According to this school of thought, the *latifundio* system and the existing land tenure relations constitute an effective brake on the growth in agricultural production. If ownership of the land is several stages removed from those who actually work the land, incentives for improvements in methods, use of modern inputs and conservation will necessarily be weak. It must be remembered also that the holding of land is an efficient defense against inflation, and it is not surprising that substantial tracts of expensive and good farm land (particularly around the large cities) are held by persons in businesses and professions other than farming.

In addition, the possibility of having effective price stimuli for agricultural production is greatly reduced by the highly unequal income distribution. Large sectors of the community whose incomes are close to the subsistence level must be protected by repressing inflation in essential goods and services. This means that some farm products will be subjected to price controls, which in turn constitute a disincentive for agricultural output.[35]

2. *Capacity to import.* The other important items in this category of the "basic" or structural factors are, first, the low level of the capacity to import and, second, its instability. On the export side, the culprit is a monoproduct (or "few-product") export system (copper in the case of Chile). The exports involved are usually primary products and therefore subject to great price fluctuations. The dependence on one or a few exports thus induces a great instability in the foreign exchange earnings and also in the public finances, whose revenues are based upon such exports to a large extent.

On the other hand, export diversification is hindered by orthodox monetary methods because of the vast disparity in the productivity of the principal exports and the rest of the economy. For example, if the productivity levels of copper are a multiple of those existing in other productive activities, it is argued that a free rate of exchange, uniform for all exports, even with a minimum of

35. See Jorge Ahumada, *op. cit.* In the case of Chile the evidence points toward a rise of relative agricultural prices during inflation. But without price controls relative prices would have risen faster. (The relative prices of some inputs for agricultural production have also increased.)

import restrictions will not be sufficiently high to give the necessary incentive for the development of other export industries.[36]

On the import side, the "structuralist" school maintains that economic development as such implies disequilibrium of the balance of payments because the income elasticity of imports is higher for the less developed countries than for the more advanced nations. In the 19th century the then developing countries had a relatively high import elasticity for primary products which permitted the less developed areas to share in the economic growth of the industrializing countries. This is no longer true today. In fact, today's advanced countries show a relatively low elasticity of imports for primary products, while the import elasticity in general of today's less developed areas is very high. This squeeze may introduce a chronic imbalance in the foreign trade of the now developing countries, at least to the extent of limiting their capacity to import needed capital goods.[37] This adds to the rigidity in the supply structure of the country and thus constitutes one of the "basic factors" underlying inflationary pressures.

In the face of these balance-of-payment rigidities it is natural that a tendency toward import substitution has developed. Import substitution as a policy has been justified on two grounds: first, that through it goods become available which otherwise could not be obtained at all because of foreign exchange shortage (or supply difficulties as during wartime); second, that import substitution investment brings with it further developmental effects which could not be obtained through imports. The basic premise of this position is that investment funds which are used

36. This argument implies, first, that the community for certain reasons prefers export diversification even if it means a lower national income than might be obtained through the expansion of the traditional raw material exports. One wonders, though, if this preference would still hold in Chile were the large copper companies not in the hands of foreigners but owned by the Chilean government. Another implicit assumption might be that the demand for the raw material exports is highly inelastic. (But if this is so then the productivity difference is not very relevant.) In the case of Chile, the demand for copper seems to have been much more elastic than was thought considering the fact that the country lost a substantial part of the world market by not encouraging copper exports between 1946 and 1954.

37. This argument is similar to one of the theses of Dr. Raúl Prebisch, Director of the Economic Commission for Latin America, as found in some of the publications of that organization. See also Aníbal Pinto, *Ni estabilidad ni desarrollo, op. cit.*, pp. 28–30.

in import substitution are not available for investments in other lines. The objective is to obtain a faster growth of gross national product than the slowly expanding capacity to import will permit.

Nevertheless, it was soon realized, even by the "structuralists," that often import substitution introduces other rigidities so that sometimes the net benefit of this policy has been difficult to assess.[38] First of all, domestic production of what was previously imported does not always reduce dependence upon imports: raw materials, machinery and other capital goods and supplies will have to be imported for the new production. In some cases this sensitizes the economy even more than the import of the finished product. Once a factory exists with substantial capital equipment and labor force it will be more difficult to let the plant and its employees become idle because of import problems than it would have been to reduce the importations of the finished product, particularly if it is not a basic necessity.

The second point of rigidity which import substitution might introduce is of course the need of protection for the new industry. If the new industry is "inefficient" from the point of view of the international division of labor, its productivity levels will be low, its prices necessarily high and permanent protection will be needed.

The third type of rigidity introduced by import substitution is the creation of monopoly structure since the productive plant for many of the substituted imports necessarily must be large relative to a restricted market such as Chile's.

3. *Distribution of income.* Another "structural" impediment for a more elastic supply of products is said to be the very unequal distribution of personal income.[39] This income distribution in itself implies a certain composition of demand both domestically and for imports, which is not conducive to a high growth rate. Domestic production and imports would cater to the restricted higher income groups. Therefore, it is argued, investment and import substitution would be geared toward such production to the detri-

38. See on this point *Desequilibrios estructurales y crecimiento industrial – El caso chileno,* by David Felix, *op. cit.*

39. On this point see *Los obstáculos al desarrollo económico,* by Horacio Flores de la Peña (Universidad Nacional Autónoma de México, Mexico City, 1955), and the writer's review of this book in the *American Economic Review,* Vol. XLVII, Number 3, June 1957.

ment of growth industries and investment in social overhead which could give greater flexibility to the economy. The negative effect of the unequal income distribution on the expansion of agricultural production through preventing a substantial betterment of relative prices in agriculture has already been mentioned.

In addition, the savings rate is exceedingly low not only because of low income levels in general but also because of a completely disproportionate propensity to consume of the upper income groups.[40] Consumption habits of this group are said to be entirely out of line with those of equivalent income groups in more developed countries. Specifically it was claimed for Chile that if the upper income groups had the same consumption pattern as their counterparts in the more advanced countries, the savings rate could be doubled.[41]

Government Finances and Public Investments

The other category of structural factors has to do with the instability of government revenues in the face of the rigidity of government expenditures. In a country where about one quarter of public income depends upon the exports of one product,[42] it is clear that public finances will be affected severely by fluctuations in the price of that product. On the other hand, current expenditures are relatively rigid, consisting principally of salaries and social security contributions. If, for some reason, public employment cannot be reduced significantly, it is clear that when revenues drop due to lower copper income, the only item that can be effectively curtailed is public investments. In addition, deficit financing may become unavoidable. The first factor, the curtailing of public investments, will be detrimental to economic develop-

40. There are some indications that the savings ratio of the middle income groups might be higher than that of the upper income groups in Chile.
41. See Nicholas Kaldor, *op. cit.*
42. The following is a percentage breakdown of Chilean government tax revenues by main sources in 1956:

	Per Cent
Copper companies	26
Customs duties	21
"Indirect" taxes (excise, sales, turnover taxes, etc.)	35
"Direct" taxes (property and income taxes)	18
Total	100

(Data from Institute of Economic Research, University of Chile.)

ment; the second, deficit financing, will create inflationary pressures.[43]

Yet institutional obstacles make it difficult to expand public revenues. Tax collection is deficient and, except for the copper revenues, the government relies heavily upon indirect taxation, which is relatively easy to administer. This makes the tax system less progressive than it could be. It not only aggravates the inequality of the income distribution but also, the argument continues, the indirect tax structure is in itself inflationary because whenever revenues have to be increased, recourse to this tax system will have a direct effect on increasing the price level.

B. *"Non-structural" Factors*

"Circumstantial" Factors

In addition to the "basic" or "structural" factors, this school of thought distinguishes "circumstantial" factors, such as exogenous import price increases, political upheavals, catastrophes and, with special emphasis, irrational government interventionism. Deficient public administration, lack of coordination and multiple and badly employed controls will all exert pressures on the price level. For instance, the "structuralists" supported the abandonment of the excessive multiple exchange rate system and burdensome import regulations which gave rise to speculation and other inflationary pressures in Chile prior to 1956.

Propagation Factors

The most important group, however, of "non-structural" forces is that referred to as "propagation" factors. The "propagation" factors are those that feed back on and aggravate the inflation problem. They arise from the capacity of the various sectors of the economy to defend their real income. Included in this category

43. See Aníbal Pinto, *Ni estabilidad ni desarrollo, op. cit.*, Section 21, pp. 51–55. The basic inflationary factor here is, of course, that revenues fall short of expenditures and not the fact of fluctuations in revenues. What is probably meant by calling the ups and downs a "structural" factor is that when there are windfall tax revenues due to, say, a good copper export price, the government immediately commits the increased revenues for salaries, social security expenditures and other items which are difficult to reduce when revenues unexpectedly fall due to, say, a sharp drop in copper export earnings.

are the credit mechanism, the automatic cost-of-living wage and salary adjustments and government deficit spending.

As already mentioned, the "structuralists" claim that orthodox monetary policy is directed only toward the propagation factors of inflation. The heart of that policy consists of a reduction of demand. The result is that the output of the most dynamic sectors of the economy, such as manufacturing industry and construction, is reduced to the level of the most backward sector of the economy, the one with the lowest elasticity of supply, which is, as in the Chilean case, agriculture.[44]

The "structuralists" admit that this policy might have worked in the past when the wage-earning sector was politically weak. But today the situation is different, because even in times of unemployment the political power of the workers is not eliminated. This means that the force of the measures attacking the propagation factors is relatively weak and they cannot be applied for long periods without causing unrest.[45]

In short, the point of the "structural" school is that an attack on the propagation factors of inflation will at best achieve a certain stability to the detriment of economic growth by reducing economic activity in the various sectors to its lowest common denominator.

44. See Aníbal Pinto, *Ni estabilidad ni desarrollo, op. cit.* p. 64. It is clear that in much of their analysis, the "structuralists," just as their "cost-push" counterparts, assume downward price rigidity in the "dynamic" sectors. In other words, if, because of a change in the composition of demand, prices in certain sectors go up, they ought to go down in other sectors. If they do not, because of a downward price rigidity, then there will be an inflationary push and unemployment. Then, if wage earners try to protect their real incomes and obtain wage adjustments and the government acts to alleviate unemployment, inflation will continue and perhaps accelerate. Anti-inflation policies of the "traditional" type will under those circumstances depress the "dynamic" sectors, that is to say, those sectors where prices are rigid downward. (Of course, absolute prices need not decline anywhere, even with price flexibility, if there is not only a change in the composition of demand but also an increase in total demand in all sectors made possible through monetary expansion.)

45. According to the "structuralists" this explains why the restraints on wage increases became milder as time wore on from the point when the orthodox stabilization policy was first applied with vigor in 1956. On the other hand, the credit line was maintained more firmly. This in itself aggravated the problem by squeezing enterprises as their costs went up in the face of restricted possibilities of borrowing further working capital.

C. *The "Structuralist" Program*

While it is relatively easy to spell out the criticism by the "structuralist" school of orthodox stabilization policy, it is rather difficult to detail its positive policy proposals. The policy objectives are rather clear, but what is the concrete economic policy recommended by the "structuralist" school? It is not easy to find a satisfactory answer in its writings or pronouncements.[46]

Attacking the "structural" factors is a multi-faced problem and, in addition, it may take time for results to appear. The "structuralists" do not wish to discard monetary policy altogether, but they believe that it must be subordinated to the objective of correcting the basic maladjustments. The picture given is that monetary policy should be used not only to hold the line until the longer-run policies can take effect but also to support the structural changes.

The result is that a rather vague picture of economic policies emerges from the "structural" line of thought. This writer is not aware of any concrete, well-defined policy proposal that "structuralists" might have put forth for the Chilean case. The lack of precision is undoubtedly due to the fact that the "structuralists" have not been in a policy-making position in that country and the formulation of a concrete program is usually relegated to a time when such a policy can be considered practically.

Nevertheless, a certain pattern of economic policies does arise from the "structuralist" position. Such a program would consist of both domestic and foreign economic policies.

In regard to the latter, the principal objective would be the lessening of the vulnerability of the economy to foreign trade. This refers both to the problem of the instability of foreign exchange income and to the fluctuations in public revenues. This vulnerability, as was pointed out before, is considered one of the basic generators of inflationary pressures.

The other measures would have to do more specifically with increasing the elasticity of supply, that is, making the supply respond faster to changes in the level and composition of demand — making resources more mobile.

46. The difficulty is that there is no coherent "structuralist" theory. It is obvious that the primary concern of the "structuralists" is economic development, not inflation. But for the process of economic development it has not yet been possible to specify a body of internally consistent mechanisms.

A third body of policies would be directed toward protecting and, if possible, increasing the real income of the masses. The motivation for the redistributing measures, according to the "structuralists," would be based not only on social and political grounds, which certainly loom very importantly, but also on economic reasons: such measures are seen to stimulate an orientation of resources toward high-priority economic activities.

Domestic Economic Policies

Probably the most important part of the program of the "structuralists" is, as has been indicated, the elimination of the obstacles toward greater flexibility in production. This aspect is directed principally toward agriculture.

Government investment in transportation, marketing facilities, irrigation and the provision of development credit and technical know-how are advocated as means to overcome the relative stagnation in agriculture. Price controls are also considered one of the factors contributing to the agricultural bottleneck, but the elimination of price controls in agriculture and a consequent improvement in the relative prices of agriculture depend upon a betterment in the distribution of income so that the purchasing power of the masses can be increased.

The present land tenure arrangements are seen as among the greatest obstacles to the growth in agricultural output. Agrarian reform, therefore, is an integral element in "structuralist" economic policy. It should not be ignored that land reform is also seen as a part of the policy designed to redistribute income and raise the purchasing power of the lower income groups.[47]

The tax system too should be revised with the design to increase agricultural production. Such an objective would also be in line with the aim of making the tax system more progressive. In this respect the idea would be to diminish the proportion of indirect taxes in favor of increasing direct taxation. Nevertheless, in view of the administrative difficulties of increasing income taxes in less

47. Too often it is assumed that the generally accepted test for agrarian reform is always economic. Many "structuralists" and "non-structuralists" would advocate land reform solely on the basis of "social justice," as long as national income does not decline too seriously.

developed areas, this would mean that property taxes should be increased. Obviously the emphasis would be on property taxes in agriculture in order to force an expansion of production in the *latifundios*.

Foreign Economic Policies

What the "structuralists" have in mind in regard to the group of measures designed to lessen the vulnerability of the economic system to foreign trade undoubtedly includes a foreign exchange rate structure designed to encourage other than traditional exports. This does not mean that a cumbersome multiple exchange rate system would be favored but it would signify a two- or three-rate system in economies where the productivity of the traditional export industries is vastly superior to their nearest competitors.[48]

The giving of incentives alone, however, is not considered sufficient; the state must attack more vigorously the problem of establishing an adequate infrastructure to make the emerging of other industries possible. And if the building of roads and other transportation means and the providing of energy, etc., is not enough, then the government should intervene to build the necessary factories or undertake the needed agricultural cultivation. This kind of industrialization and agricultural development would work both ways, to increase and diversify exports and to reduce import requirements.

In regard to reducing the instability of fiscal revenues due to foreign trade fluctuations, several measures have been put forward. One would be that the government should establish a stabilization or contingency fund when foreign trade income is high. In the case of Chile for instance, if copper prices are above those foreseen in the government budget, the excess tax revenue would go into this special fund. In bad years the fund could be drawn upon in order to meet the necessary government expenses not covered by the lower tax revenues.

Because of lack of confidence in the fortitude of the public administration which is necessary for such a scheme to be successful,

48. A differential tax system which could accomplish the same thing without introducing multiple exchange rates is also recommended by some "structuralists."

a stronger measure is sometimes proposed.[49] The burden of stabilization would be shifted to the copper companies. A minimum tax on copper exports would be levied which would be based upon the average production and prices over, say, a given five-year period. When copper exports fell below this average, the companies would have to pay the minimum tax, but they could deduct the excess taxes paid in that year from the tax liability in years when their export value was above the average. The revenue received over the minimum would be used by the government for export diversification, economic development in general, or be destined for a stability and contingency reserve. Such schemes would be combined with measures to reduce the proportion of fiscal revenues deriving from foreign trade.

The Chilean "structuralists" with few exceptions ignore the question of foreign aid. This is probably a reaction to what they consider an excessive preoccupation of the last Chilean governments with outside financial help as a means to resolve all economic problems. Other "structuralists," however, recognize the need for foreign aid. In a letter to the author the Mexican economist Víctor Urquidi underlines the role of such assistance in making possible the carrying out of an anti-inflation policy which attacks the structural factors.

Monetary and Fiscal Policies

Monetary policies and also fiscal policies are complementary in this program. They should be geared to create the conditions to obtain the desired changes in the structure of production, government finance and volume and direction of investment. One of the basic assumptions in this respect is that qualitative credit controls are possible and must be introduced.

Nevertheless, in this view the expansion of money must be kept passive, that is to say, in step with any increase in the cost of output. If money is kept completely passive, permanent inflation will result unless costs are being restrained. Credit controls in the private sector of the economy would have to be tightened whenever

49. See Chilean Senate document containing proposed bill on "Nuevo trato a los trabajadores," by deputies Albino Barra, Ramón Silva, Mario Palestro and Alfredo Hernández, January 9, 1959, pp. 7–8. See also Aníbal Pinto, *Ni estabilidad ni desarrollo*, *op. cit.*, pp. 78–80.

the government sector was forced to increase its borrowing for necessary purposes.

Here it is interesting to point out that the "structuralists" do not necessarily favor massive cost-of-living wage and salary adjustments and in their pronouncements have frequently insisted on the desirability of restricting wage and salary increases, with the proviso, of course, that this would be politically feasible only if positive economic development measures were taken at the same time.

In general, the "structuralist" position is that the investment rate can and must be increased. Orthodox anti-inflation policy dictates that planned investments should be reduced to equal planned savings. Development policy, however, should have the opposite objective, that is, increasing the rate of savings. In the thinking of the "structuralists" this is possible because the unequal distribution of income means a great concentration of disposable income in the hands of the few, whose savings could be increased substantially.[50] If ordinary incentives fail to raise the propensity of the rich to save (or invest), then the "structuralists" would certainly want the government to tax the upper income groups in order to finance an increase in public investment.

IMPLICATION FOR A SOCIO-ECONOMIC POLITICAL SYSTEM

It is obvious that the "structural" program requires the state to exert new efforts in the guidance of the economy. It is to intervene directly through substantial increases in public investment not only in the traditional "overhead" sectors but also, if need be, in industrial and agricultural activities. The objective is not socialization but rational application of government action. Even in classical economics, the "structuralists" say, there are certain areas in the economy that are conceded to the state and in adolescent economies there surely must be room for substantial responsibility by the state over the available resources and over the fiscal, monetary and foreign trade instruments.

The "structuralists" put greater emphasis on proper coordination of government action because they realize that the careless interventionism of the past, with its contradictory control systems, has often aggravated the problems it tried to solve. They blame

50. See Nicholas Kaldor, *op. cit.*

the recent inclination toward laissez faire in some quarters of the Latin American community to just such experiences of irrational state intervention.

The basic assumption for the "structural" program, of course, is that the political conditions exist to make possible the carrying out of the objectives without crippling opposition. Within the practical framework of Latin American politics this raises the fundamental question about reality in these countries. Is the assumption realistic that in a less developed area the government would have sufficient administrative skill and sophistication to manage refined and highly complex tools in a difficult process of coordination to bring about a compatibility of economic development with stability? And even if the government could muster the necessary administrative and technical skills to manage such a program, would it also be capable of commanding a political majority without sacrificing democracy?

Or is it more realistic to assume that a laissez-faire policy will bring the necessary adjustment in the economy to make possible the emergence of new dynamic forces? Would the application of monetary policy bring results of stability sufficiently fast to clear the way for new spurts in private investment? Or would such adjustments, if they do take place, require so long a time as to last beyond the breaking point of the endurance of the now socially conscious masses with the consequent danger of violent upheavals?

There is a basic difference in political feasibility between the "structural" program and orthodox monetary policy. Monetary policy is a relatively efficient economic tool in politically unwieldy or intractable situations. "Structuralist" policies require for their success under democratic conditions firm political support even of those whose vested interests are endangered by the intended changes.

Therefore, a primary objective of the "structuralists" in the implementation of their difficult long-term program is to create a national consciousness and an almost religious spirit for economic development.[51] In this manner it is hoped to create the conditions

51. See for instance, Luis Escobar, "Necesidad de una interpretación nacional del desarrollo económico," *Economía*, Facultad de Ciencias Económicas, Universidad de Chile, No. 67, second quarter 1960; Aníbal Pinto, *Ni estabilidad ni desarrollo, op. cit.;* Celso Furtado, *op. cit.*

that will make possible cooperation from all sectors of the community and will bring forth the needed sacrifices by all groups: the sacrifice of additional consumption by the great masses of the community; the sacrifices that are entailed in agricultural reform, tax reform and a greater government role in general for the landowning and business groups.

The emergence of a nation-state alone, however, is often not enough to create this necessary spirit for the development push. In many instances national fervor for common objectives and actions can be aroused only through the appearance of national emergencies such as war or warlike conditions or through the creation of an image of a common enemy, in the form of imperialism, colonialism or the like.

If the needed "spirit" is not forthcoming, we face a situation in which the groups in power within the existing socio-political framework have the ability to bring forth the necessary changes but are not, according to "structuralists," really interested in them. This is the great dilemma of political reality which is posed by the "structuralist" school.

In Chile the need to face this dilemma may be postponed temporarily because the country is now faced with a tremendous reconstruction problem arising from the earthquakes and tidal wave catastrophes of 1960. The government, whether it likes it or not, would necessarily have to take a more "structuralist" line because in the minds of the people reconstruction naturally takes precedence over stability in this emergency. A partial test of the compatibility problem between monetary stability and the injection of dynamism into economic activity will take place in this country when (and if) reconstruction gets into full swing. This test might not be sufficient to either vindicate or discredit the "structuralist" school. Therefore, the settling of this policy conflict in Chile may be postponed for a while longer, at least until the catastrophe-induced sense of urgency wears off. But accelerated economic development must be part of such a settlement. It would be too much to expect from a populace whose economy has been close to stagnation for several years for it to bear the consequences much longer without its patience wearing thin, even where the relatively sophisticated Chilean masses are concerned.

THE MOVEMENT TOWARD REGIONAL TRADING GROUPS IN LATIN AMERICA

by Raymond F. Mikesell

EARLY EFFORTS TO ACHIEVE CLOSER ECONOMIC RELATIONS

The developments which have resulted in the negotiation of the Montevideo Treaty for a Latin American Free Trade Area and of the several Central American treaties for the establishment of a common market are the product of a number of economic and political forces which have existed for more than a generation of Latin American history. Although there have been efforts to achieve political integration by various groups of Latin American states extending back for over a century, serious efforts to achieve closer economic relations between Latin American countries date from the latter part of the 1930's. During the 1930's most South American countries adopted exchange and trade controls, and some of them engaged in a deliberate effort to achieve self-sufficiency in a wide range of manufactured commodities, in order to offset the effects of reduced foreign exchange income brought about by the world-wide depression. Industrialization advanced more rapidly in Argentina than in other South American countries, and partly as a consequence, Argentina became a prime mover in seeking to achieve some form of regional trading arrangement with neighboring countries which would provide a broader

Raymond F. Mikesell is W. E. Miner Professor of Economics at the University of Oregon. The author traveled in Latin America in the summer of 1960 and is in part reporting on the opinions he encountered in the course of many talks with Latin American officials and economists.

market for her manufactures. Thus in 1939 Argentina and Brazil negotiated a treaty of industrial complementation and free commerce, and in 1941 Argentina proposed a customs union of the Plata which would include a number of bordering countries.

During the 1930's several South American countries employed clearing agreements and other means of bilateral balancing in trade between themselves as well as in their trade with Western Europe. However, the problem of financing trade between South American countries was not satisfactorily dealt with, and it was not until well into the 1940's that Latin American countries began to negotiate European-style payments agreements among themselves which provided for a reasonable degree of flexibility, including swing credits. It is interesting to note that the 1940 draft treaty for the establishment of an Inter-American Bank provided facilities for the multilateral compensation of balances within Latin America.[1] This treaty, which was drawn up in Washington largely by U. S. financial experts, was never ratified.

In the immediate post-war period, a network of bilateral trade and payments agreements was developed which linked together the non-dollar countries of South America. There were also renewed efforts on the part of Argentina to achieve economic integration with its neighbors. These efforts were undoubtedly inspired in part by Peron's desire to extend Argentina's political influence, but there was also a strong economic basis for the expansion of trade opportunities, particularly in industrial products. This interest was not limited to the Southern Zone countries. An agreement was reached in Quito in 1948 among Colombia, Ecuador, Panama and Venezuela for the establishment of a customs union, but the treaty was never ratified. In fact, none of the ambitious efforts on the part of the South American countries to achieve economic integration during this period came to fruition. Economic nationalism and political disputes were simply too strong to permit the realization of economic integration goals.

THE ROLE OF ECLA

The interest in expanding regional trade within Latin America, and in finding a solution to the payments problem, was reflected

1. For the text of this treaty see the *Federal Reserve Bulletin,* June 1940.

in the activities of the United Nations Economic Commission for Latin America shortly after its organization. In 1948 ECLA adopted resolutions for the study of a Latin American customs union and payments union. In 1949 ECLA requested the International Monetary Fund to study the possibility of establishing a regional mechanism for the multilateral compensation of bilateral balances. The report of the IMF was not favorable to the establishment of a Latin American multilateral clearing mechanism, and suggested that "the effort involved would most certainly be out of proportion to the benefits received."[2]

This report was not well received by the countries of the Southern Zone of South America nor by ECLA. The action of the United States in providing generous support to the European Payments Union, while taking a negative attitude toward a payments arrangement for Latin America, was regarded as further evidence of U. S. discrimination and neglect of Latin America's problems. On the other hand, some of the dollar countries of Latin America tended to side with the United States on the question of the desirability of a special payments mechanism for Latin America.[3]

The Central American Agreements

During the period 1951–56 ECLA conducted a number of studies of trade and payments relationships among Latin American countries, but its activities in promoting regional trade arrangements were confined very largely to the Central American countries.

Central American leaders have long been aware that their opportunities for industrialization and for attracting industrial capital were extremely limited in the absence of the creation of broader

2. See *Multilateral Compensation of International Payments in Latin America,* United Nations Economic and Social Council, E/CN/.12/87, May 27, 1949, p. 33.

3. For an excellent review and analysis of the events leading up to the establishment of the Montevideo Treaty see Víctor L. Urquidi, *Trayectoria del mercado común latinoamericano,* Centro de Estudios Monetarios Latinoamericanos, Mexico City, 1960. See also "The Emerging Common Market in Latin America," *Monthly Review,* Federal Reserve Bank of New York, September 1960.

markets. Beginning in 1951 El Salvador negotiated bilateral free trade agreements with four neighboring countries – Nicaragua (1951), Guatemala (1951), Costa Rica (1953) and Honduras (1954). But these agreements were limited to a few commodities and were not very effective in promoting trade. In response to a 1951 resolution of the Commission, ECLA organized the Committee of Economic Cooperation of Central America, which played an important role in the long-drawn-out negotiations on the multilateral agreements for free trade and economic integration in Central America. In June 1958 five Central American countries – Costa Rica, El Salvador, Guatemala, Honduras and Nicaragua – signed an "Agreement on the Regime for Central American Integrated Industries" and a "Multilateral Treaty on Central American Free Trade and Economic Integration." The Integrated Industries Agreement, which provided for joint planning and certification of manufacturing firms in particular industries, which would be given free access to the Central American market, reflected ECLA's philosophy of planned integration, as opposed to free entry and competition, in the achievement of economic integration. The Multilateral Free Trade Agreement provided for the elimination of duties on some two hundred commodity groups and for the eventual establishment of a customs union. The 1958 Central American agreements were ratified by only four countries, Costa Rica having failed to do so.

Early in 1960, with some technical assistance from the United States, three of the Central American countries, El Salvador, Guatemala and Honduras, negotiated a new treaty for a free trade area which would eventually become a customs union. This treaty, which was far more liberal than the earlier treaty involving five countries, was apparently negotiated quickly and without the assistance of ECLA. More recently, however, ECLA has gotten back into the picture and has assisted in the negotiation of a new treaty called a General Treaty on Central American Integration. This treaty, which has been signed by El Salvador, Guatemala, Honduras and Nicaragua, is a consolidation of the other treaties. In addition, these countries have signed a Protocol which provides for a uniform tariff on a large number of items. Finally the four nations have signed an agreement for the establishment of a

Central American Bank for Economic Integration, which is expected to be financed in part by the U. S. government.

The Latin American Free Trade Area

The developments in Western Europe in the mid-1950's stimulated a renewed interest in the creation of regional trade agreements in Latin America. As the European Common Market began to take shape, Latin Americans became increasingly concerned about the possibility of losing their markets to African producers of coffee, cocoa and bananas. They felt that only a strong regional economic organization could deal effectively with discrimination from this source.

In 1956 there was created within ECLA a Trade Committee charged with the task of formulating specific plans for regional markets within Latin America. During the period 1957–59 a series of meetings were held under ECLA auspices, some attended by experts acting in their private capacities and others by governmental representatives, working along three different lines. First, consideration was given to the development of a Latin America-wide free trade area or common market. Second, a Central Banks Working Group was created to consider payments problems in inter-Latin American trade, and in particular to formulate a scheme for the multilateral compensation of bilateral payments positions arising out of existing bilateral agreements. Third, committees were formed to plan for the creation of regional free trade areas or customs unions within Latin America.

During this period ECLA was presented with something of a dilemma. First, ECLA desired to avoid the setting up of regional trading groups within Latin America which would inevitably involve discrimination between Latin American countries. In addition, ECLA was anxious to capitalize on the strong political movement toward Pan-Latin Americanism. For some time, Latin Americans had been emphasizing the desirability of greater political coordination, but as yet had found no means of expressing in a concrete way this desire for greater political unity. On the other hand, ECLA realized that rapid progress toward economic integration could only be made by regional groups, such as that constituting the Southern Zone of South America, and the Central

American countries. ECLA sought to solve this dilemma by the appointment of a Working Group of experts under the chairmanship of former President of Ecuador, Dr. Galo Plaza, and including well-known representatives from the major Latin American countries, to draw up a proposal for a Latin American free trade area which would somehow be consistent with the independent development of regional free trade areas or customs unions. The results of the endeavors of the Working Group, which were carefully guided by Dr. Raúl Prebisch, the Executive Secretary of ECLA, were embodied in the report of the second session of the Working Group meeting in Mexico City in February 1959.[4] These proposals were noted and, for all practical purposes, shelved, at the Panama City meeting of ECLA in May 1959.

Meanwhile, events moved rapidly during 1959 and 1960 toward the creation of what started out to be a Southern Zone regional free trade area agreement. Although the initial meetings of the government representatives for the establishment of a regional free trade zone were held under the auspices of ECLA, subsequent meetings following the meeting in Santiago of representatives of Argentina, Brazil, Chile and Uruguay in April 1959 showed some waning of ECLA influence and a taking over of the project by the government representatives themselves. At the September 1959 conference in Montevideo, which included representatives of Argentina, Bolivia, Brazil, Chile, Paraguay, Peru and Uruguay, and observers from Mexico and Venezuela, the basic provisions of the Treaty of Montevideo were drafted and in February 1960 the Treaty of Montevideo establishing a free trade zone encompassing Argentina, Brazil, Chile, Mexico, Paraguay, Peru and Uruguay was signed by the government representatives, followed in April by the installation in Montevideo of the Provisional Committee of the Latin American Free Trade Association.[5]

4. At the suggestion of the U. S. State Department, the second session of the Working Group included an independent U. S. member, the present writer, whose reservations on the Working Group proposal were published as an annex to the report in a document entitled *The Latin American Common Market,* United Nations, Department of Economic and Social Affairs, 1959, p. 50.

5. Bolivia requested an extension of time for signing the Montevideo Treaty as a founding country, and will probably join the Association.

The inclusion of Mexico as a signatory to the Treaty, which came as something of a surprise, eliminated the regional character of the Association and undoubtedly doomed ECLA's plans for a Latin America-wide agreement which would encompass regional trade associations. If the movement toward a free trade area in Latin America is to grow, it will grow by reason of additional countries joining LAFTA rather than by the creation of several regional organizations (other than the Central American group) which would, according to ECLA's plans, have been united under a Latin America-wide agreement. Colombia and possibly Ecuador are likely to join LAFTA shortly after it has been officially established, and their adherence will spell the end of efforts to create a regional trade organization encompassing the Gran Colombia countries.

Although the Montevideo Treaty is in many ways a child of ECLA and reflects many of ECLA's basic ideas, there is considerable evidence that ECLA is not altogether satisfied with the product. Moreover, ECLA will not be able to dominate the policies of the Association. ECLA does provide technical assistance to the Provisional Committee in Montevideo, but the Committee determines its own policies. According to Protocol No. 3 of the Montevideo Treaty the Pan American Union was also to provide technical assistance to the organs of LAFTA, but the Union has not established close working relations with the Provisional Committee.

Although ECLA has not taken an official position which is in any way critical of the provisions of the Montevideo Treaty, many ECLA officials are concerned with some of the provisions of the Treaty. Foremost among these is the lack of automatic arrangements for reducing tariffs on commodities not now traded among the members of LAFTA. Some thought that the Treaty would need to be amended in the direction of a customs union so that significant margins of tariff preference could be assured. ECLA officials are also concerned that more progress has not been made toward a solution of the payments problem. ECLA continues to favor some kind of arrangement for the multilateral clearing of bilateral balances along the lines of the recommendations of the Central Banks Working Group. However, my discussions with the governmental representatives of member countries revealed that the majority of them prefer to do nothing about the payments problem in the expectation that payments between Latin American countries will eventually be put on a convertible basis. This position is in line with the movements toward convertibility following the monetary reforms in Argentina, Chile, Paraguay and Uruguay. Also, the currencies of Mexico and Peru are fully convertible.

BUSINESS INTERESTS AND ATTITUDES

In considering the forces leading to the negotiation of the Montevideo Treaty, one should not overlook the vigorous support given by influential economists and business leaders in a number of countries who have reached the conclusion that industrial development in Latin America cannot proceed at a rapid pace without a broadening of the markets for manufactured commodities. Foremost among these enthusiastic supporters are José Garrido Torres, until recently head of the Superintendencia of Money and Credit in Brazil, and the author of a number of articles on the desirability of a Latin American common market; Flavián Levine, Executive Vice President of Chile's largest steel company and professor of economics at the University of Chile, who has also written widely on this subject; Galo Plaza, former President of Ecuador; and Rodrigo Gomez, Director General of the Banco de Mexico. A number of industries, particularly in Brazil and Mexico, have substantial excess capacity for the production of automobiles, durable goods and various types of capital goods. Business leaders in these new industries are generally favorable to the creation of a free trade area. Moreover, government and business leaders are aware of the fact that the production of many substitutes for imports on an economic scale is not feasible without the possibility of exports.

At the present time the Mexicans are the most enthusiastic supporters of LAFTA. The Banco de Mexico has a large staff (some forty professionals) doing research on various aspects of inter-Latin American trade, and Mexico is the only country that has met the request of the Provisional Committee in supplying an official list of commodities which it would like to export to South

America. (Argentina has supplied a provisional list.) The Mexican Chamber of Commerce has sent a delegation to visit groups of businessmen in other Treaty signatory countries, and there seems to be relatively little opposition in Mexico to the scheme. The major Mexican labor organizations have also supported Mexico's ratification of the Treaty.

In the course of hearings before joint sessions of three committees of the Mexican Senate, outstanding representatives of business, of banking and of labor interests in Mexico all emphasized the necessity of creating broader markets for Mexico's industrial output as a means of stimulating industrialization and increasing productivity.[6] In addition to testimony from representatives of Mexican business associations, labor organizations and leading banks, there was also testimony from several government officials. Although it was recognized that Mexico must import more from other Latin American countries if she is to expand her exports to Latin America, the witnesses were eager to point out to the senators that individual industries, and, of course, agriculture, were not going to be hurt. For one thing, many of the imports from other Latin American countries would constitute a diversion of trade from the United States and Western Europe. Any idea that a Latin American free trade area would involve open competition with Mexican products was certainly soft-pedaled. Some of the senators were concerned about the problem of duplication of investment within the free trade area arising out of the operation of the Treaty. It was suggested that so far as possible the Association would promote joint planning of economic development so as to avoid duplication and encourage a fair and economical utilization of the resources of the region. There was also emphasis on planned adjustments in industries affected by the move to freer trade.

While there is some enthusiasm in Brazil, representatives of some of Brazil's older industries, in particular the textile industry, have voiced considerable fears regarding the Montevideo Treaty.

6. *Versión taquigráfica de las audiencias para el estudio del Tratado de Montevideo* (mimeo.), Hearings before Joint Sessions of the Committees of Foreign Affairs, Foreign and Domestic Commerce, and Customs and Foreign Commerce of the Mexican Senate, October 10–17, 1960, Mexico City.

On the other hand, most Brazilians believe that their competitive position in manufactures within the free trade area is quite strong and tend to explain the conservative nature of the Montevideo Treaty on grounds that without the various escape clauses, Brazilian products are likely to flood the Latin American market.

In my discussions with a few Argentine business and government leaders, I gathered that only in the textile industry is there outright opposition to the Treaty, while the Argentine Industrial Society is wholeheartedly supporting it. One of the Society's executives, Mr. Anthony Blank, serves as a kind of traveling salesman and promoter for the free trade area throughout Latin America.

In Chile the only industrial group that appears to be quite active, both in research and in the promotion of LAFTA, is the steel industry under the leadership of Flavián Levine, who heads the Chilean Steel Institute. Although many Chilean businessmen see advantages in the creation of a regional free market, they are concerned about their competitive positions because of a widespread feeling that the escudo is substantially overvalued.

In Peru, business attitudes ranging from apathy to outright fear are found. By and large few people have given the free trade area or the problems which it raises a great deal of thought. Only a few far-sighted and progressive businessmen, like Juan Pardo Heeren, former Minister of Finance and son of an ex-President, are actively campaigning for the free trade area. Peru is likely to ratify the Treaty more for political reasons than from any support from the business community.

The attitude of the business community in the three less industrialized signatories to the Treaty, namely, Peru, Paraguay and Uruguay, is one of great skepticism as to what is in it for them. They see little hope of exporting industrial commodities to the more industrially advanced countries, and express considerable fear of having their industries hurt by heavy competition from the more industrially advanced countries. On the other hand, staying out of LAFTA has dangers too, since it might involve in some cases discrimination against their agricultural exports. However, they do not expect to receive much in the way of advantages for their agricultural or primary commodity exports in the light of the special escape clauses for agriculture.

ANALYSIS OF THE PROVISIONS OF THE MONTEVIDEO TREATY

The following analysis of the Montevideo Treaty and of its probable operation is based on discussions with ECLA officials, government officials in member countries, including members of the Provisional Committee, and with private economists and business and banking officials.

A review of the provisions of the Treaty reveals many ideas and approaches which have been developed by the ECLA literature on regional trade programs. Foremost among these are the principle of reciprocity, and the principle of complementarity, which are to be achieved through joint planning and industrial integration agreements. However, it would be wrong to assume that these ideas originated with ECLA, or that in the absence of ECLA direction these countries might by themselves have developed a truly liberal free trade treaty. In fact, there is considerable evidence to indicate that the Montevideo Treaty is less liberal and more conservative in terms of the number and kinds of escape clauses than the ECLA Secretariat would have liked. Thus, the extremely conservative approach reflected in the Free Trade Area Treaty, its de-emphasis of international competition, and its emphasis on planned trade and trade balancing, is in very large measure a reflection of the attitudes of most of the governments whose representatives negotiated the Treaty. ECLA's main function was to provide the initiative for the negotiation of the Treaty, and to articulate and provide the rationale for the basic positions held by the government representatives. It should be remembered, however, that governmental attitudes in some Latin American countries are changing rapidly and that economic philosophies differ substantially between government officials in Latin America both between countries and within the same country.

Mechanism for Tariff Reductions

Unlike the European Economic Community Treaty or that establishing the European Free Trade Association, there are no automatic, across-the-board provisions in the Montevideo Treaty for moving toward the complete elimination, or even the substantial removal, of all barriers to actual or potential trade among the members of LAFTA. The Treaty was drawn with the deliberate intention of making it unnecessary for any member to make a reduction in its tariff or other barriers with respect to any particular import, or even to undertake a *substantial* reduction of the *average* level of duty or other barriers on its imports, as a matter of compliance with the Treaty obligations. In fact, I was told that the introduction of automatic provisions requiring drastic changes in the level of import barriers would have been unacceptable to the signatory countries. Therefore, the Montevideo Treaty must be viewed very largely as a mechanism for conducting reciprocal negotiations for the reduction of tariffs in accordance with certain principles laid down by the Treaty.

Article 2 of the Treaty provides that the free trade area "shall be brought into full operation within not more than twelve years from the date of the Treaty's entry into force." How can this provision be squared with the other provisions of the Treaty? This is done, in effect, by a simple statistical device. Article 5 provides that "each contracting party shall annually grant to the other contracting parties reductions in duties and other charges equivalent to not less than 8 per cent of the weighted average applicable to third countries, until they are eliminated in respect of substantially all of its imports from the area . . ." However, a careful examination of the formula established in Protocol No. 1 of the Treaty for calculating the reductions in the weighted average of restrictions applicable to intra-LAFTA trade reveals that member countries only need to reduce their restrictions on the commodities that they are already importing from other members in substantial volume. Since this trade is largely of a non-competitive nature and is limited very largely to agricultural commodities not being produced in adequate quantities in the importing countries and non-agricultural primary materials and fuels, the required reduction in the average tariff can be brought about without the admission of any new products and with very little disturbance to the pattern of trade. Moreover, since the Treaty contains very liberal escape clauses, which make it unnecessary for any member to liberalize its imports of agricultural commodities from other members to the point where its domestic producers would be significantly affected, even the bulk of the intra-group trade is left outside of the required liberalization process.

Trade in manufactures constitutes less than 5 per cent of intra-LAFTA member trade, and about a third of this trade is represented by semi-processed copper manufactures. Most of the trade in non-agricultural primary commodities, which constitutes less than 5 per cent of total intra-LAFTA trade, is not likely to be affected significantly by a reduction in tariffs. Hence, it is clear that most, if not all, members of LAFTA could reduce their average tariff on imports from the other members by 90 to 95 per cent in accordance with the formula established by the Treaty – which presumably would represent substantial compliance – without reducing restrictions on manufactures or on other commodities which might involve competition with domestic producers. This again is because of the overwhelming weight in the determination of the weighted average of tariff duties on intra-LAFTA trade given to duties on those commodities which are either subject to the agricultural escape clauses or are not likely to be affected significantly by changes in restrictions. The major hope for a substantial expansion in intra-LAFTA member trade, therefore, lies in the negotiation of concessions on manufactured goods and perhaps some agricultural commodities which have not been previously traded in significant quantities. Thus, the actual achievement of a free trade area depends upon the course of negotiations on concessions affecting commodities in the national schedules, and on agreements for placing commodities in the common schedule.[7]

The idea of employing a system of averages for reducing tariffs – as against across-the-board reductions in all duties – has been prominent in ECLA reports on the subject, and was included in the recommendations prepared by the Mexico City Working Group of February 1959. However, the ECLA recommendations, while permitting substantial flexibility as to the particular tariff rates which would need to be reduced in order to achieve the target reductions in terms of averages, provided for a division of

7. Article 4 of the Montevideo Treaty provides for (a) "national schedules specifying the annual reductions in duties, charges, and other restrictions which each contracting party grants to other contracting parties . . ."; and (b) a "common schedule listing the products on which the contracting parties collectively agree to eliminate duties, charges, and other restrictions completely so far as intra-area trade is concerned . . ." within the twelve-year period.

the products into three categories, namely, primary goods; capital goods, motor vehicles and other durable goods; and manufactured goods for current consumption — with minimum reductions established for each category. Moreover, the ECLA Working Group recommendations did not contain the formula embodied in Protocol No. 1 of the Montevideo Treaty, which had the effect of limiting the required reductions entirely to goods currently being traded. For this reason it may be said that the Montevideo Treaty is far less liberal as regards the requirements imposed upon members for achieving a reduction in duties than the recommendations embodied in the ECLA reports. In fact, it was the intention of the formula suggested by ECLA that the required reductions would apply to goods, particularly manufactures, not currently traded in significant volume.

The absence of automatic requirements for across-the-board reductions of restrictions on commodities actually or potentially entering into trade constitutes a grave disadvantage, if not an effective barrier, to the achievement of a free trade area. The tariff negotiators will be subject to strong pressures from within their own countries not to grant concessions on commodities which are actually being produced in the home market, or on commodities which they expect might be produced within the foreseeable future. It has been suggested that all commodities not being produced in any member country in significant quantities should be put immediately into the common schedule, and duties and other restrictions on such commodities be removed either immediately or within a relatively few years. Such action would provide a powerful stimulus to both foreign and domestic investment. Unfortunately, however, this suggestion is not likely to be adopted, since most countries are not willing to give up the right to establish new industries and to afford them protection, except, perhaps, in return for an important concession from other members on a commodity that they would like to export.

In discussing the process of negotiation with government officials in various countries, it was clear that members do not contemplate making concessions on commodities which they are producing in sufficient quantities to supply all or a substantial proportion of their domestic requirements, or expect to do so in the foreseeable future. Continuation of this attitude, of course, could result in there being an extremely limited range for bargaining with respect to national schedules, and the inability to find agreement on more than a few commodities to be placed in the common schedule. National attitudes, of course, might change when government and business leaders see that little progress in expanding exports can be made without making concessions which will affect some domestic industries. But the experience of GATT negotiations has been that import protection interests are much more powerful than those interests seeking to expand exports.

The Principle of Reciprocity

A basic principle which appears frequently in the Montevideo Treaty is the "principle of reciprocity," a concept which is also current in the ECLA literature on regional trading arrangements. According to this principle, each country will negotiate concessions on import restrictions with the expectation that the concessions given and received will result in a more or less equal expansion of that country's exports and imports in trade with other members of the area as a whole.

The underlying reason for the inclusion of the principle of reciprocity is twofold. First, it is basic to the principle which ECLA as well as several of the member countries have maintained in the past, namely, that inter-Latin American trade should not give rise to balances which must be settled in gold or convertible currencies. It has been a firm belief of ECLA that at least the Southern Zone Latin American countries would never agree to a trading arrangement which resulted in a country's having to settle a balance in convertible currencies. The argument is analogous to the "dollar shortage" argument which was quite common in Europe several years ago. In effect, it argues that since Latin American industrial products are not competitive with U. S. and Western European products, any country receiving convertible currencies in payment for an inter-Latin American surplus would spend the funds outside of Latin America. The second underlying reason is that no country should receive a benefit to its own industrialization program as a consequence of increased industrial exports at the expense of a limitation on the industrialization of other members. Since it is expected that negotiations on concessions will be largely concerned with industrial products, the principle is to achieve a kind of "balance of industrialization" within the LAFTA area.

How is this principle going to be applied in practice? It will obviously be impossible to determine with any degree of exactitude just what would be the effect of proposed concessions on the trade balance of any individual country. The consensus seems to be that if in the year or two following the initial negotiations on concessions, a country increased its imports from the group substantially more than its exports to the group, adjustments would need to be made either through reintroducing restrictions or through obtaining additional concessions from other countries. In this way members would attempt to restore a balance in the additional trade brought about by the concessions, in the following period.

The principle of reciprocity is likely to constitute a very serious limitation on the expansion of trade among members of LAFTA, and probably an insuperable barrier to the eventual achievement of a free trade area. Basically this principle assumes that the expanded trade with the group as a consequence of trade negotiations can be balanced for each member, and that such balance would constitute a normal condition for members of a free trade area. But given freely competitive conditions and the absence of restrictions on intra-area member trade, there is only the slightest chance that each country's exports (or additional exports) would be even approximately balanced by its imports (or additional imports) from the group as a whole. Adjustments are more likely to be made in the direction of restoring restrictions on the part of countries incurring deficits than through the granting of additional concessions by countries experiencing surpluses. In this connection it is worth noting that Article 8 of the Treaty specifically provides that "concessions granted in respect to products which appear only on the National Schedules may be withdrawn by negotiations among the contracting parties and on the basis of adequate compensation."

Competition vs. Planned Complementarity

A significant feature of the Treaty lies in the absence of any statement on, or provision for, the achievement of market competition within the area. The term "competition" does not appear any place in the Treaty, nor is any recognition given to the existence of business practices both within countries and between firms in different countries which may tend to stifle competition. This is certainly in line with ECLA's negative attitude toward competition in favor of regulation, planning and government operation, but it is firmly rooted in the attitudes and practices of most Latin American governments. The concept of competition is certainly not a respected one in Latin America, and the idea that freer inter-Latin American trade would stimulate efficiency and productivity by breaking down some of the barriers of government-sponsored or -sanctioned monopolies is, to say the least, not a motivating factor behind the creation of a free trade area. On the other hand, there is recognition of a need for greater complementarity between the industrial sectors of individual Latin American countries.

Although for some years ECLA has stressed in its publications the desirability of import substitution as a means of dealing with the problem of increased demand for imports in the face of stagnating or slowly rising foreign exchange incomes, in the past few years a feeling has arisen that substitution and a broadening of the industrial base is impossible for individual countries with limited markets, and that the solution to this problem must be found in broader markets and specialization within Latin America or among the countries of particular regions. Of course, one of the reasons why there has been a lack of complementarity between industrial sectors of different Latin American countries has been the virtual absence of trade in industrial commodities. The Treaty suggests, however, that this complementarity shall be achieved by planning and the negotiation of complementarity agreements, rather than through the operation of competitive market forces.

The complementarity articles of the Treaty are exceedingly vague, but discussions with government and industrial leaders have revealed some of the types of arrangements which they have in mind. For example, it is hoped that certain parts and intermediate goods for the production of automobiles and tractors might be produced in different countries, with each country perhaps continuing to assemble its own finished product. Certain grades and types of steel products would be made, say, in Chile, some in Brazil, some in Argentina, on the basis of government-sanctioned private agreements and permission for trade. The idea of industrial integration agreements, such as that embodied in the Central American treaty for a system of integrated industries, in which member countries would agree to establish an industry or a branch of an industry in one country which would be permitted to market its product in the other member countries without competition for a period of time, has also been discussed. However, one gets the impression that there has been little real planning in this area and that the road to achieving planned complementarity will be a long and difficult one.

One of the difficulties in seeking to apply the principle of planned complementarity as against competition exists in the differences in economic philosophies found in the governments themselves. There appears to be a rather strong move in Argentina and Chile toward greater freedom for private enterprise, both domestic and foreign. The new Quadros government in Brazil may also favor a greater degree of freedom in business and the elimination of private monopolies. If complementarity is to be achieved by means of private agreements, which would amount to international cartel arrangements, such agreements either will need to be subject to a high degree of governmental control or they are likely to be in opposition to consumer and general public interests. There is a real danger that cartel agreements will tend to stifle progress toward greater productive efficiency and the expansion of production and trade within the area.

Escape Clauses in the Montevideo Treaty

The operation of the averaging formula, the principle of reciprocity and the special provisions concerning agriculture constitute in themselves such a broad departure from the principles of a free trade area that additional specific escape clauses such as are provided in Articles 23–26 would seem to be quite unnecessary to protect member countries against unforeseen developments in their trade with one another. The inclusion of these articles provides additional opportunities for the withdrawal of concessions or the adoption of new restrictions for a broad range of purposes. For example, Article 23 authorizes a contracting party to impose restrictions on imports of products included in the liberalization program (including items in the Common Schedule), "if these products are imported in such quantities or under such conditions that they have or are liable to have serious repercussions on specific productive activities of vital importance to the national economy." This Article would appear to permit a country to impose restrictions whenever any important industry feels itself injured or likely to be injured by competition from producers in other member countries.

Article 24 authorizes a contracting party "which has adopted measures to correct its unfavorable *over-all* balance of payments to extend these measures, provisionally and without discrimination, to intra-area trade in the products included in the liberalization program." Since nearly all members of LAFTA have been chronically in a condition of disequilibrium and are likely to require balance-of-payments restrictions of some kind in order to avoid a drain of exchange reserves, this provision could probably be used by most members to justify restrictions on trade in products included in the liberalization program. It is difficult to see why such a provision should have been included *in addition to* the withdrawal of concessions permitted under Article 8, in accordance with the reciprocity principle. Thus, for example, why should a country whose exports to the Area have increased more than its imports from the Area be permitted to impose restrictions on imports from the Area because its *over-all* balance-of-payments position was unfavorable? It is true, of course, that according to Article 26 the Committee is empowered to request any contracting party which maintains such balance-of-payments restrictions for more than one year to enter into negotiations with a view to eliminating the restrictions. But the fact that a contracting party can take unilateral action and adopt measures which can remain in operation for at least a year before it is even obligated to discuss the propriety of such measures with the Committee, provides little hope for effective action by the group in preventing an unwarranted use of restrictions for balance-of-payments purposes.

These escape clauses, together with the reciprocity provisions, have the effect of making any concession or liberalization measure with respect to a product, whether that product be on a national list or on the common list, little more than temporary action which can be revoked at any time for a variety of reasons. Thus, the liberalization measures are not sufficiently permanent to give a prospective domestic or foreign investor within the area the confidence he requires to undertake an investment to supply a market in other LAFTA members. It is understandable, of course, that some provision for temporary action to prevent an unexpected flooding of the domestic market or a serious balance-of-payments disturbance would need to be included in the Treaty. But such actions should be carefully limited and should not be taken without the consent and continuous scrutiny of the Committee. As presently drafted, it is difficult to see how the existence and operation of the Treaty can have an appreciable effect on the pattern of investment, especially in the private sector.

Most-Favored-Nation Treatment Clause

Article 18 of the Montevideo Treaty constitutes a fairly straightforward and unequivocal statement to the effect that any advantages either existing or as a result of the trade liberalization program, which are granted to any other country by a contracting party, shall be immediately and unconditionally extended to the similar product originating in, or intended for consignment to, the territory of other contracting parties. Article 19 does provide an exception in the case of arrangements for facilitating border trade, but this is a quite justifiable and traditional clause in Latin American most-favored-nation agreements. There are a number of situations in which the border passes through communities in which the residents on either side of the border have more in common with one another from an economic standpoint than they do with other regions in their own country.

The most-favored-nation treatment clause takes on special significance because there are in existence between signatories to the LAFTA Treaty a number of bilateral agreements involving important discriminatory concessions, such as, for example, the elimination of exchange surcharges on imports into Argentina from Chile and Brazil. Assuming that these agreements are not denounced, a multilateralization of these concessions as required under Article 18 may be of considerable significance.

While it was obviously the intention of the drafters of the Treaty to eliminate discrimination arising out of the usual type of concessions made under a trade liberalization program, it is by no means clear how this principle can operate in the case of special complementarity agreements. In some cases these complementarity agreements may involve private agreements between firms in two countries, the agreements having been sanctioned by the governments. Such agreements would include, say, the right to import specific manufactured commodities which may constitute intermediate products or portions of product lines of an industry, in exchange for the right to export complementary products to private firms in the other country. Planned complementarity arrangements of this kind simply do not lend themselves to the application of the most-favored-nation treatment principle. The existence of state trading and of monopoly import privileges among members also raises questions with respect to the operation of the most-favored-nation treatment clause. Often state trading is accompanied by bilateral agreements with other countries. But unless state trading operations are conducted solely on the basis of the commercial principles of buying in the cheapest market and selling at the best prices, state trading practices must inevitably violate the most-favored-nation principle.

The provisions for special assistance to the less industrialized countries also violate that principle. Chapter VIII of the Montevideo Treaty provides that the contracting parties may authorize the extension of concessions by some contracting parties to other contracting parties at a relatively less advanced stage of economic development within the area which are not extended to other contracting parties. It also authorizes a contracting party at a relatively less advanced stage to proceed more slowly with its liberalization program. These provisions, which involve discrimination and the possibility of special deals which violate the most-favored-nation principle, were taken over from the recommendations of the ECLA Working Group.

The Montevideo Treaty and GATT

GATT has never been popular with ECLA, nor for that matter is it revered in Latin America generally. At the time of the GATT negotiations in Havana in 1948, Latin American members argued strongly for the inclusion of the right of less developed countries to adopt tariff and quota preferences among themselves. This principle was denied, although the South American countries have generally practiced the principle, justifying it either on balance-of-payments grounds or on grounds that it constituted "border traffic." ECLA has consistently argued that the GATT provisions were loaded in favor of the industrial countries since there exist broad escape clauses for primary commodities, including agricultural products, enabling the industrial countries to place quantitative barriers on imports from the less developed countries, but the less developed countries are supposed to abide by the GATT rules regarding imports of industrial commodities. There is considerable justification in this criticism, as was pointed out by the Haberler report, *Trends in International Trade* (GATT, Geneva, October 1958). In spite of these feelings toward GATT, it is quite evident that the four LAFTA signatories that are members of GATT (Brazil, Chile, Peru and Uruguay) have no intention of leaving GATT and are anxious to have the LAFTA Treaty sanctioned by GATT as a free trade area coming within the conditions for such arrangements laid down by GATT. In addition, Argentina has recently taken initial steps toward becoming a member of GATT.

Recently the Provisional Committee in Montevideo undertook to answer some 250 questions submitted by GATT members regarding the Montevideo Treaty and its operation. Although many of the questions could not possibly be answered until after the Treaty goes into operation, the answers could not resolve some of the basic inconsistencies between the Montevideo Treaty and the free trade area provisions in GATT. For example, it is obviously impossible to show how under the terms of the Treaty, with tariff reductions based on negotiations under the principle of reciprocity and with the agricultural and other broad escape clauses, the elimination of barriers to substantially all trade could be accomplished within the twelve-year period. In addition, the Treaty says nothing about the maintenance of discriminatory quantitative restrictions against non-members.

It seems clear that the governments of LAFTA members do not expect any serious opposition from the United States or from major Western European countries to the Montevideo Treaty. In fact, in the light of the very liberal interpretation of the GATT rules with respect to the Coal and Steel Community and the European Free Trade Association, Latin Americans would be highly indignant if there were any serious opposition. For political reasons it is most unlikely that the United States will raise serious questions regarding the agreement, and the Latin Americans know it. In a sense the Treaty provides official sanction for the principle of a discriminatory arrangement which falls far short of a free trade area or customs union within GATT – something the Latin Americans have been arguing for for years!

The Problem of Payments Arrangements

In many ways the problem of payments and the settling of bilateral balances under payments agreements has been a basic factor in efforts to achieve regional economic integration in Latin America. As has already been noted, ECLA and the governments of the Southern Zone were concerned with this problem and with the possibility of creating some kind of multilateral payments mechanism long before there was any serious discussion of the creation of a free trade area or common market. Had the Montevideo Treaty been negotiated five years earlier, it probably would have been accompanied by some kind of multilateral offset or clearing scheme along the lines of that worked out by ECLA and the Central Banks Working Group. But by 1959 most of the member countries were committed to monetary reforms involving a high degree of freedom of exchange transactions so that a payments regime based on inconvertible currencies appeared to be out of step with the current trend. ECLA, however, still pressed for an automatic payments arrangement along the lines of the now defunct European Payments Union, but this was vigorously opposed by the IMF and the U. S. government. This opposition, plus the commitment of Argentina, Chile and other countries to the IMF for currency reforms, doomed the ECLA proposals, and at the time of the Montevideo negotiations the whole question of payments was conveniently shelved by referring it to the Central Banks Working Group for further study. This does not mean that many business and government leaders are not concerned about the payments problem, but the achievement of anything along the lines of an automatic clearing of inconvertible balances is probably out of the question. There is perhaps greater concern over the problem of additional liquidity in financing transactions and even more concern over the problem of intermediate credits for the financing of goods in inter-Latin American trade in competition with the liberal credit facilities being offered by U. S. and European firms with the aid of government-sponsored credit and credit-guaranteeing institutions.

AN EVALUATION OF THE MONTEVIDEO TREATY

Experience with international agreements has shown that the detailed provisions of treaties are not the most important factors in the successful realization of the broad purposes of the agreements. Even an ideal treaty providing for completely automatic reductions in duties and with the most carefully drawn and limited escape clause provisions would not guarantee success if political and economic conditions generally were unfavorable and if governments lacked the will to carry out their obligations in terms of the spirit as well as the letter of the agreement. Thus, for example, it is doubtful whether we would have a world of freely convertible currencies had the Articles of Agreement of the International Monetary Fund been approved without the inclusion of an indefinite transition period and certain other broad escape measures. On the other hand, we must be aware of the limitations of the Montevideo Treaty in evaluating the likely nature of its accomplishments. Moreover, broad statements of purposes, such as the creation of a free trade area and regional economic integration, do not have the same meaning for all countries or regions. Hence we must look closely at the provisions of the agreement in order to understand how the countries represented at the Montevideo Conference envisage its operation and its accomplishments.

In evaluating the agreement it must be kept in mind that trade and other economic transactions between countries can be no freer than similar economic activities within countries. The continuation in Latin America of a substantial degree of direct government participation in economic life, plus a very large amount of government regulation and influence in economic activities, both official and unofficial, provides a much different framework for a free trade area or common market than exists, say, within Western Europe. To take an extreme case, a common market among a group of socialist countries scarcely has the same meaning, if indeed it has any meaning at all, as a common market among countries where production and trade are largely in private hands.

It seems clear that the signatories to the Montevideo Treaty did not have in mind the creation of a broad regional competitive system in which governments would no longer play an important role in production and trade. They do realize the need for broader markets and for a better allocation of their investment resources. They also realize that with slowly growing external markets for primary products, they must broaden their export base to include industrial commodities. But since they fear that they cannot compete with the older industrialized countries, they must create preferential markets for their own industrial goods. Thus by means of regional specialization and trade, they can produce a wider variety of commodities on an economic scale and thereby limit the rapid growth of their import requirements from the rest of the world.

The recognition that narrow economic nationalism cannot deal successfully with the problems of economic growth, even with substantial external assistance from the United States and international organizations, constitutes a significant development in Latin American thought. Speeches and articles by Latin American economists and government officials favorable to the free trade area have constantly emphasized the relationship of broader markets and *planned* integration to economic development. The regional integration movement is not an expression of a conversion to the doctrine of free trade and competition. Moreover, except for the hope that regional commodities can displace imports from the rest of the world, thinking about the Treaty and its operation tends to look toward the future as it affects the pattern of investment. This, of course, is consistent with the generally accepted principle that existing industries should not be hurt by competition from other members as a consequence of the granting of tariff concessions.

The principles according to which regional integration is to be planned are clearly indicated in the principles of reciprocity and complementarity found so frequently in the Treaty. Just how planned regional integration is to work out in practice is much less clear, however. The Treaty does not provide for an institution to coordinate investment programs among the various members.

Unlike the proposed Central American integration program, there is no provision for a system of "integrated industries" under which the establishment of firms in certain industries is to be jointly planned. Except possibly for special complementarity agreements between members, coordination of investment programs can only take place or be influenced through tariff negotiations.[8] If countries are to obtain concessions which will help them to expand their exports of certain commodities, they must expect to give concessions on other commodities. Presumably they would give concessions on commodities the production of which the government did not intend to encourage. In other words, decisions reached in the process of the tariff bargaining would reflect, to a degree at least, the development programs of member countries.[9]

It is difficult to predict just how much economic complementarity can be achieved under the Treaty as currently interpreted. The economic and political obstacles to negotiating substantial concessions covering a large proportion of the commodities that might be potentially traded within LAFTA are immense. A great deal depends upon the strength of the member governments over the next decade, since weak governments are not likely to expose their position further by tariff concessions which might alienate politically important groups. The difficulties in applying the principle of reciprocity or equal gains in exports may very well constitute a barrier to a significant reduction of restrictions. Still another obstacle is to be found in the problem of payments, the solution for which is by no means in sight.

With all of its shortcomings and within the context of national economic policies in Latin America, the Montevideo Treaty is certainly a step in the right direction. In time some of these shortcomings might be overcome, either by amendments to the Treaty or by the members' adoption of liberal policies which go beyond the requirements of the letter of the Treaty's provisions. Conceiv-

8. Officials in some member countries are known to favor common regulations with respect to foreign investment so as to avoid competitive bidding for investments by firms which would market their products in the free trade area.

9. In discussing this question with a high official of Nacional Financiera, Mexico's government-controlled development bank, I was told that this institution was already taking into account the possible results of tariff negotiations in its own investment decisions.

ably new organizations or means of coordinating development programs may be created. After all, the Montevideo Treaty constitutes the first important concrete step taken by Latin American countries themselves for dealing cooperatively with their common economic problems.[10] Thus, given time and reasonable political stability, the Montevideo Treaty is an encouraging sign that Latin American countries will be able to cooperate in the solution of some of their most fundamental problems in achieving satisfactory rates of economic growth. But there remains the question whether the pace of events in this vital field of economic cooperation is too slow to meet the urgent demands of the social revolution which is shaking with increasing violence the economic and political structure of every country south of the Rio Grande.

10. Although the coffee-producing countries of Latin America have gotten together on a commodity agreement with respect to the marketing of coffee, this is not a problem which all Latin American countries have in common.

THE COMMON MARKET AS A TOOL OF LATIN AMERICA'S ECONOMIC DEVELOPMENT: A COMMENT

by VÍCTOR L. URQUIDI

ECONOMIC change in a foreign country has usually been judged by its effect on one's own country rather than in the light of the benefits sought by the inhabitants of the country in question. It is therefore very encouraging, after a long period in which many Latin American countries have undertaken policies

Víctor L. Urquidi is Economic Adviser to the Bank of Mexico and a member of the Colegio Nacional de México.

that were looked upon with disfavor by the major trading nations of the world, to find that much recent writing on the region has begun to focus on the real issue, namely, the widely felt need for more rapid and comprehensive development, particularly through industrialization. Latin American trade policies favoring this new trend are better accepted than before. Social reform – from improved land tenure to taxation of high incomes – is today urged not only by social scientists but also by governments at inter-American conferences. Perhaps Latin American monetary and banking policies, still a doctrinal black sheep in foreign eyes, may also in the future be comprehended and regarded more sympathetically. There is, in the United States and elsewhere, a growing realization that Latin America is fighting a desperate battle against poverty and that there are certain objective conditions, over which Latin American countries have no control or which change only slowly, that make the region's task more difficult than it would seem from historical analogy to other parts of the world, or from the often facile recommendations of international experts.

Professor Mikesell's paper is an important contribution to the study of what lies ahead in one aspect of future growth: the expansion of inter-Latin American trade. But in unravelling and analyzing the particular manner in which the region is seeking closer integration within itself, he says little – perhaps understandably, since he is confined by his immediate subject matter – about the basic economic development problems. Nevertheless, these are still the primary preoccupation of government leaders, business and labor organizations, economists and others in Latin America. Regional integration, and the accompanying trade arrangements – whether a free trade zone or an eventual common market – are but a part, albeit a very important one, of the broader problem of economic growth.

Despite Latin America's size and a population greater by about 20 million than that of the United States, something about the nature of past economic development has not been quite satisfactory. Let it be granted that for reasons of climate, resources, population and social and political antecedents, productivity in the United States might have been expected to be higher. Still, Latin America's real income per head is little more than one-ninth of the American average, and even in those Latin American countries that are less underdeveloped, or in certain advanced areas within them, the standard of living barely exceeds one-fourth the United States standard and one-half the Western European.

In seeking the origin of this situation, at least one stark fact must be accepted — that in Latin America, capital is generally scarce and expensive. Much of the groundwork for development is still non-existent, and some basic installations have become run down. Highways, ports, power plants and dams have to be built, and railroads rehabilitated and extended. Even where some of these facilities are adequate, they are not always fully and properly used. Scarce resources also have had to be tied up in industrial plants that often operate below capacity and at high cost to the consumer. Technological research and training for higher skills are barely beginning to expand. Education and sanitation are as yet privileges of a minority. To compound these difficulties, as against a small and not always optimally used stock of real capital and low levels of productivity, Latin America has, unfortunately at this stage, the highest rate of population growth of any region in the world. It is, therefore, wrong to let the pressure of this population build up without endowing it with adequate capital resources, or to wait for its purchasing power to develop "naturally." On the contrary, great efforts have to be made to achieve a rapid transformation of the economic and social structure in the Latin American countries, involving accelerated capital formation, improved productivity and less inequality of income and wealth.

This, then, is the development problem, as seen today, whether for one country or for all Latin America combined. The Treaty of Montevideo addresses itself to one aspect of the problem: can development be undertaken better, or sooner, by creating conditions for freer trade among the Latin American countries rather than leaving each country to its own devices? It is tempting to wonder whether Latin America's economic growth in the past might not have been more rapid if instead of today's twenty separate customs territories there had been a single one from the beginning of independence or shortly thereafter. Would industrialization have started earlier in such a case? But these questions can hardly be answered, because, among other things, economic policies and thinking up to the 1929 depression were dominated by the simple proposition that certain leading countries were destined to become industrialized and other areas, like Latin America, were meant to be suppliers of raw materials. Since 1930, the expansion of world demand for the export products of the underdeveloped countries has slowed down (except in wartime) and in turn, not unrelatedly, areas like Latin America have been engaged in becoming industrialized in a deliberate manner. The ideas and policies of today are different, and so are many of the basic conditions.

When mention is made of industrial development in Latin America, it should be remembered that a new stage is now well in sight. Light consumer goods industries exist in most countries, and they meet the bulk of current demand for wage goods; there would be no difficulty, either, in expanding these industries as demand increases. The modern clamor for home appliances and similar durables has also been met in part through assembly plants, and now in some countries by means of a high degree of domestic manufacture. Iron and steel, pulp and paper, basic chemicals, building materials and other intermediate products are among the most rapidly growing manufacturing industries in the region. The new stage of Latin American industrialization is that imposed by the machine age. Metal-transforming and tool-making industries have taken hold in a number of countries and are expanding, thus laying the foundation for the manufacture of machinery and equipment of many kinds, including electrical, agricultural and transport equipment. A promising start is also being made in the automobile industry and its component parts.

It could be argued that Latin America may be attempting to compress too many stages of industrial growth into one. However, there are compelling reasons for this new policy. First of all, there is no particular economic logic in proceeding gradually from the simple to the complex; the merest consideration of inter-industrial relationships is enough to show that different manufacturing branches are interdependent, and the same holds true as between industrial and agricultural development. Secondly, the rapid rate of increase in rural population requires an over-all rate of industrial growth sufficiently large to absorb present underemployment and enable further shifts of people from the land into manufacturing as higher productivity per worker is achieved in agriculture. Thirdly, Latin America's ability to earn foreign exchange from the rest of the world is seriously limited by the slow expansion in the over-all demand for basic products and by frequently violent price fluctuations. According to an estimate made by the ECLA Secretariat, export proceeds from basic commodities over the next fifteen years or so may not grow by more than an average of 3 per cent annually.[1] Some countries face a better prospect and others a worse one. But, also, most countries are highly dependent on two or three commodities and heavily subject to market fluctuations. It has been further estimated by the ECLA Secretariat that such a rate of increase in exports could not sustain a moderate rate of growth of real income — of, say, 5 to 6 per cent annually — unless the growth of imports is kept in line and a substantial amount of long-term capital is made available to Latin America. In order to prevent a slowing down of capital formation and essential consumption while permitting imports to increase only within limited foreign exchange availabilities, there is no alternative but to expand manufacturing in Latin America on a vast scale, not only to meet ordinary consumption needs but to supply increasing proportions of the region's demand for intermediate products, durables, and industrial, agricultural and transport equipment.

If the above reasoning is correct, this new, higher stage of industrial growth requires broader markets than those afforded by the customs territory of any individual country. An acceleration of economic development in Latin America, especially through further industrialization, and the expansion of intra-regional trade are thus mutually dependent processes.

As Professor Mikesell points out in his paper, these ideas are increasingly gaining the support of business leaders, labor organizations and government officials throughout Latin America. This largely explains the relative speed with which specific proposals were worked out to launch Latin American economic integration. It is important to realize that the move toward the development of a free trade area under the Treaty of Montevideo was not inspired by the traditional theory of international trade and specialization and the resulting considerations about customs unions. The ultimate purpose is not to free intra-regional trade as such, with whatever unhampered allocation of economic resources may result, but

1. Cf. ECLA, *The Latin American Common Market,* Part B, "The influence of the common market on the economic development of Latin America" (United Nations Publication No. 59.II.G.4).

to reinforce mutually the process of economic development in the region. It is not the purpose, either, that some Latin American countries should become economic colonies of others. It should surprise no one that the framework provided for in the Treaty does not happen to fit a theoretical free trade model, or correspond to the European Common Market procedures, or adapt itself literally to the provisions of GATT that were drafted thirteen years ago under quite different circumstances. Neither should it be expected that a group of Latin American countries that are essentially mixed economies with varying degrees of state ownership, controls and public planning alongside the largely uncoordinated private sector, would suddenly and immediately engage in complete laissez-faire trade among themselves. Professor Mikesell recognizes this toward the end of his paper – although, in the light of his previous analysis of the Treaty, probably with some reluctance.

If Latin America is to speed up its rate of economic development, over-all programming must undoubtedly play a vital role. In this context, it is difficult to believe that intra-regional trade should be left to chance. There certainly should be, and undoubtedly will be, ample scope for the growth of unplanned intra-regional transactions; nevertheless, it is quite likely that much of the major expansion of trade will be the result of carefully worked out arrangements, which in turn will partly condition some of the important industrial developments. It may be that a consideration of the problem from this angle could do much to dispel the concern of Professor Mikesell (as well as of others who have written on the subject) with the non-automaticity of many provisions in the Montevideo Treaty.

It is yet too early to forecast how far the first round of negotiations among the members of the Latin American Free Trade Association in 1961 will promote an immediate increase in trade. On the other hand, despite the arguments of Professor Mikesell and others to the contrary,[2] there is nothing in the Treaty, or in the intention of the member governments, to suggest that currently non-traded

2. E.g., the article entitled "The Emerging Common Market in Latin America" in the *Monthly Bulletin* of the Federal Reserve Bank of New York, September 1960, and T. E. Sumberg, "Free Trade Zone in Latin America," *Inter-American Economic Affairs,* Summer issue, 1960; cf. also my comment on the latter in the following issue, pp. 19–27.

commodities, namely, a vast array of manufactures, will fail to be negotiated to enter progressively into the computation of the annual average reduction of 8 per cent in the intra-zonal tariff. Trade in manufactures is already increasing moderately without awaiting the coming into force of the Treaty. The commodity lists drawn up by nearly all the member governments at this date and proposed for negotiation include, at the urging of business and industrial interests, hundreds of items in iron and steel, chemicals, equipment and machinery. If the Treaty were not concerned with these products, it should never have been signed. Private enterprise in Latin America is evidently much more alert to profitable trading opportunities than outside observers might surmise, and the response of Latin American industry so far shows that the vision of the economists and the government officials involved has been more than justified.

Professor Mikesell overstresses what he feels are the shortcomings of the Montevideo Treaty to the point of presenting it almost as an instrument for the consolidation of private cartels and government monopolies. He finds not only that the attitude of ECLA (and, presumably, of the Latin American governments as members of this body) toward competition is "negative," but fears that the safeguarding provisions of the Treaty will be used to stifle competition. He even states rather broadly that "the concept of competition is certainly not a respected one in Latin America." But it would be well to define this concept. Monopolistic proclivities and practices, and fiscal protection, are present everywhere, not only in Latin America; it is a question of degree. The issue in the case of a Latin American free trade area should not be judged on doctrinal grounds or on the basis of presumed attitudes, but against the background of the entire and complex set of development problems. The competitive spirit is not as defunct as Professor Mikesell suggests, and though resistance from vested interests may be expected, it is unlikely that, under a process of rapid growth of demand and reciprocal "demonstration effects," tight monopolistic situations will prevail, individually or through cartelization. On the other hand, to throw the doors wide open to the extent of imposing drastic readjustments on a particular country would be self-defeating. The safeguards and escape clauses in the Treaty are thus necessary, although it should be noted that they are subject to scrutiny and that the intention, expressed throughout, is to expand, not restrict, intra-regional trade.

It should not be overlooked, either, that the Treaty establishes most-favored-nation treatment among its signatories, which means that if country A obtains a tariff reduction on commodity X from country B, this concession is also granted by the latter to countries C, D, etc. Every member of the free trade association will actually compete in the market of the country that makes a concession on a particular trade item; each member opens up its market to all the others. Despite the obviously necessary exceptions to this rule as regards border traffic and existing bilateral commitments, the free trade area is therefore competitive on this count also.

Space does not permit commenting on a number of Professor Mikesell's other points on which interpretation may differ. But a few words are called for, first, as regards the relation of the Montevideo Treaty to GATT and, secondly, with respect to the role played by ECLA in the development of a Latin American common market.

The situation vis-à-vis GATT is encouraging. At different stages of negotiation, the four Latin American countries interested in the free trade area that were also members of GATT maintained informal contact with the latter, and, as the proposals evolved, the issues were discussed in detail. Information was given to the Contracting Parties at GATT's fifteenth session in 1959, and detailed questionnaires were answered during 1960. More recently, at the sixteenth session of GATT held last November, authorization was given to proceed with the application of the Montevideo Treaty, in general accordance with Article XXIV of GATT, subject to further clarification of legal and practical aspects as the Latin American Free Trade Association develops and expands. It thus appears that there is a basic understanding and that the free trade area in Latin America, similarly to regional arrangements in Europe, is not objected to by the major trading nations.

ECLA has played an essential part in the movement toward a Latin American common market. Both ECLA's able Secretariat and some of the Latin American governments took the lead in 1955, and a systematic exploration of ideas was carried out. The recommendations of many outside experts were carefully taken into account. What emerged finally in Montevideo was not overambitious but realistic, and it can encompass as many Latin American countries as may wish to join. The thought of an all-embracing integration agreement among the twenty countries, or of the prior formation of several subregional groupings (other than the precarious one in Central America), did not receive sufficient support from governmental opinion. These other possible solutions can hardly be said to have been ECLA's "plans," as Professor Mikesell puts it, nor can ECLA be surprised and "not altogether satisfied with the product," nor chagrined at not being "able to dominate the policies" of the Free Trade Association. It was and is the role of ECLA as an inter-governmental United Nations Regional Commission to make recommendations to its member governments, and of ECLA's Secretariat to make appropriate studies and assist the governments in formulating their policies. These respective roles do not prevent governments, however, from acting as they consider in their best interests. When Mexico and Peru decided to participate with the original four Southern countries in the Free Trade Association, and recently Colombia and Ecuador announced their intention of joining, it was because they felt, together with the other members, that it was a good policy for themselves and for Latin American economic development. At the governmental level, ECLA and the Montevideo Association should have no difficulty in conciliating the differences of opinion; at the Secretariat level, ECLA's cooperation will undoubtedly continue to be invaluable, though its views are not necessarily operative or binding on the Montevideo group. Much work remains to be done, particularly as to the position of the Latin American countries that are not signatories of the free trade area, and as to payments problems, differential tariff levels, and so on, in which it is hoped that the ECLA Secretariat and other regional technical bodies will usefully take part, in accordance with their mandate.

Several writers have expressed much skepticism over the eventual success of the Montevideo Treaty. The present comments, on the other hand, are admittedly on the optimistic side. Time will obviously tell whether there will be a snowball effect in the growth of intra-Latin American trade. Such trade is today barely 10 per cent of the region's total trade, and the members of the Association account for only one-half of it. In any case, the prospects of the free trade area cannot be judged by some preconceived standard. The Treaty of Montevideo can become a powerful instrument for accelerating trade and development. Latin America's attempt to enlarge, with all the necessary safeguards, the scope of its markets as an aid to its economic development is certainly a worthy one, and it must be judged by its results. Let us hope that these are not meager, and realize as well that Latin America's future ability to trade with the rest of the world will be greater to the extent that the free trade area is successful.

THE LAND REFORM ISSUE IN LATIN AMERICA

by THOMAS F. CARROLL

There is no doubt . . . that sweeping changes in Latin-American land-tenure systems are inevitable. Only one question remains to be answered. How will these changes come? By bloody revolution or by long-range democratic planning?
– Chester Bowles in the *New York Times Magazine,* November 22, 1959

THE land reform issue, which only a few years ago was under a sort of taboo in Latin America, has rapidly moved to occupy a key position among the policy problems of the region. The Cuban land reform, introduced in 1959 as one of the main props of the revolution, has dramatized both the necessity for overhauling existing land tenure systems and the ideological and power struggle inherent in such changes. Nowadays, land reform problems are vigorously debated throughout Latin America and there is a proliferation of projects and proposals in almost every country. While the issue is extremely complex and has many po-

---

Thomas F. Carroll is a staff member of the Food and Agriculture Organization of the United Nations and is currently serving as Regional Officer for Land Tenure and Settlement in the FAO's Latin American Regional Office in Santiago, Chile. The views and opinions expressed by the writer are personal and do not in any way represent the policy of the FAO. *The writer is grateful to Resources for the Future Inc. and to the University of California for having enabled him to devote some time to thought and research on these problems as a visiting member of the Economics Department at Berkeley. Dr. Solon Barraclough and Ing. Romilio Rodriguez read the manuscript and offered helpful comments.*

litical aspects, the principal interest of economists has centered on the relationship between land reform and development. The purpose of this essay is more modest: it is to sketch with broad strokes the agrarian situation that calls for changes, to review some of the recent attempts at reforms or those currently in progress, and in the light of past experience to advance some ideas on how continued pressure for land reforms is likely to affect policy-making in Latin American countries.

Amidst all of its inherent complexity, the core of the land reform problem is relatively simple and can be stated in straightforward terms: The existing pattern of land tenure (i.e., ownership and control over land resources) is such that it corresponds neither to the aspirations of the rural population nor to the requirements of rapid technological progress. What this usually means in action is redistribution of landed rights in favor of the cultivator, and greater social control over land resources.[1] Such changes are now being advocated both by politicians wishing to capitalize on growing popular sentiment and by intellectuals interested in modernization of their countries' institutions. Economic developers are becoming increasingly aware of the key role of agriculture in Latin American economic growth and there is a tendency to look more closely at the land tenure system as a major factor in the stagnation of the farm sector. What gives the land reform issue its peculiar fascination, however, is the income redistribution aspect. Land reform, if it is seriously done, implies a drastic re-

1. The concept of land reform is itself a controversial and semantically intriguing topic. Its narrowest and traditional meaning confines it to land distribution. A broader view includes in it other related changes in agricultural institutions, such as credit, taxation, rents, cooperatives, etc. The widest interpretation makes land reform practically synonymous with all agricultural improvement measures – better seeds, price policies, irrigation, research, mechanization, etc. The writer is of the opinion that land tenure is the central problem in land reform and agrees with the view put forward by Doreen Warriner, in her brilliant series of lectures at Cairo (*Land Reform and Economic Development*, National Bank of Egypt, 1955), that we should "not confuse the definition of a concept with the conception of a policy. To use the term land reform in this wide sense [i.e., a change in all agrarian institutions] confuses the real issues. The redistribution of property in land is a very difficult change to carry through, far more difficult and controversial than the other measures, and we cannot really put it on the same level as other institutional improvements. The order of magnitude is too different, and we take the edge off it if we ignore this fact."

arrangement of property rights, income and social status. In some ways, therefore, every reform is revolutionary.

AGRARIAN STRUCTURE

In looking at the agrarian structure in Latin America what is most striking is the great concentration of ownership in relatively few large units, and the vast number of very small units at the other end of the scale. While it is difficult to generalize for so large and varied a region, the tenure systems have much in common in most countries. Broadly speaking, the main features of the agrarian structure are: (1) the importance of *latifundios,* or very large farms; (2) the large number of *minifundios,* or very small farms; (3) the special situation of the *comunidades,* or communal holdings; and (4) the peculiar form of farm labor known as the *colono* system. A knowledge of the principal features of each system and the main problems it represents is essential in order to understand what is supposed to be "reformed."

The Latifundio

Let us first consider the large farms and their importance. As practically all the statistics are in terms of management units (*explotaciones*) rather than ownership units (*propiedades*), the degree of concentration is usually even greater than the data indicate. A few figures will illustrate this concentration.[2] In Guatemala 516 farms (0.15 per cent of all farms) represent 41 per cent of the agricultural land. In Ecuador 705 units (0.17 per cent) include 37 per cent of the farm land. In Venezuela 74 per cent of the farm acreage, comprising 6,800 units (1.69 per cent of all farms), is in holdings of over 1,000 hectares. Half the farm land in Brazil is in the hands of 1.6 per cent of the owners. In Nicaragua 362 owners have control over fully one-third of the agricultural acreage. The most extreme concentration could be observed in Bolivia prior to the land reform; there 92 per cent of the land was in fewer than 5,500 units, representing 6.4 per cent of all farms.

These figures, based mostly on census data, are of course not

2. Most of the quantitative information in this paper is based on the extensive mimeographed Spanish documentation prepared for FAO's Second Latin American Seminar on Land Problems, held in Montevideo, Uruguay, in November–December 1959.

exact, yet they give a good indication of the magnitude of land concentration. If it were possible to calculate cultivated or cultivable land by farm sizes, the index of concentration would diminish, as many of the large units include mountain, desert or swampland of doubtful value. On the other hand, it is generally acknowledged that for historic reasons the *latifundios* include the best land in most of the countries, a fact which from the standpoint of quality tends greatly to increase the land monopoly. Census counts, moreover, are usually short in the small-farm category, so that the *minifundios,* worked frequently by squatters and migrant cultivators, are underestimated. Therefore, the true percentage position of the large units is likely to be even greater.

A rapid summation of the available data yields the figures shown in Table 1 for Latin America as a whole. Roughly 90 per cent of the land belongs to 10 per cent of the owners. This degree of concentration is far greater than that in any other world region of comparable size.

Much has been written about the historic origins of the *latifundio* system. Basically, it reflects the organization of society in Spain and Portugal at the time of colonization, and the superimposition of this pattern on native cultures through large land grants.[3] The *latifundio* pattern has two main variants: the *hacienda* type of extensively cultivated estates, and the intensively worked plantations. They give rise to quite different problems and call for different measures of reform.

The *hacienda* is typically a livestock-cereal operation, with very low capital investment and labor applied per unit of land area. Ownership is often of the absentee type and labor is provided by the *colono* system or one of its variants. While there are notable exceptions, the *hacienda* system is a paragon of inefficiency both on the firm level and nationally. Output per man and per land unit is low. The plantation, on the other hand, generally shows a high capitalization combined with stricter labor organization and controls. As a result, output per land unit is generally high, and farm efficiency is above average. However, both systems em-

3. For an excellent description of the origins of the Latin American tenure system see David Weeks, "The Agrarian System of the Spanish American Colonies," *Journal of Land and Public Utility Economics,* May 1947, pp. 153–68.

TABLE 1

ESTIMATED PERCENTAGE DISTRIBUTION OF LAND HOLDINGS IN LATIN AMERICA, AROUND 1950

Size of Farms (hectares)	*Per Cent of Farms*	*Per Cent of Land Area*
0–20	72.6	3.7
20–100	18.0	8.4
100–1,000	7.9	23.0
Over 1,000	1.5	64.9
Total	100.0	100.0

Source: Based on the very helpful regional summary provided by Oscar Delgado in his *Estructura y reforma agraria en Latinoamerica,* prepared for the Sociedad Económica de Amigos del País, Bogotá, 1960 (mimeographed).

body monopoly elements, both result in extreme maldistribution of income, and in social conditions which have often been described as deplorable. The plantation problem is complicated by some foreign ownership and management, especially in the Caribbean area. But perhaps the worst feature of land concentration is the resulting concentration of power which in innumerable ways infuses the whole structure of society. It is against this concentration of power that most of the fury of popular land reforms has been directed. It is the destruction of *latifundismo* rather than other more positive goals, such as "family farming" or better land use, that provides the emotional and political mainspring of future reforms.

The Minifundio

Now let us look at the other end of the scale. The great majority of the farms are small, often so small that at the present levels of technology these *minifundios* cannot give the farm family an acceptable minimum level of living. In Guatemala 97 per cent of all farms are in units of less than 20 hectares. The corresponding figure for both Peru and Ecuador is 90 per cent, for the Dominican Republic it is 95 per cent, for Venezuela 88 per cent and for the private sector of the Mexican farm economy 88 per cent. In Colombia some 325,000 farms average ½ hectare, and a further half a million farms average 2½ hectares.

The gravity of the *minifundio* situation is increased by fragmentation, by illegal occupancy (squatting) and by shifting cultivation. In many areas (especially in the Andean mountains) these small holdings have become subdivided as a result of population pressure into tiny plots, often only a few feet wide. Métraux reports, for example, that in the Conima region on the eastern shore of Lake Titicaca there is not a single holding that is not broken up into fifteen or twenty plots.[4] Many of the smallest units are operated by squatters on either public or private land who hold no title and whose farming operations both from the point of view of security and use of resources are extremely unsatisfactory. Finally, there is the problem of migrant or shifting small-scale agriculture, practiced in vast areas of usually forested land in the tropical belt, mostly accompanied by burning and other wasteful methods. The vast majority of *minifundios* represent a hand-to-mouth type of farming and are outside the market economy.

The origin of the *minifundios* also goes back to colonial times, when land grants were "bestowed on the lower order, the conquering armies or upon civilians of humble rank."[5] Some of the more recent ones are homesteads conferred upon or sold to colonists who settled in frontier regions. Some are the result of simple occupancy, which may or may not have been confirmed legally. The extraordinarily rapid growth of population in recent decades has aggravated the *minifundio* problem both through further subdivision by inheritance and through spontaneous migration into new areas. The owners or occupants of small plots of land are beset by many problems. Many are at the margin of the market economy and represent neither a producing force of farm commodities nor an effective demand for industrial products. They generally lack not only land but other inputs necessary to raise productivity. Their plots are frequently exhausted and eroding. Institutional services, schools, roads, hospitals, are conspicuously lacking in *minifundio* areas. The peasants are at the mercy of

4. Alfred Métraux, "The Social and Economic Structure of the Indian Communities of the Andean Region," *International Labour Review*, Vol. 79, No. 3, March 1959, pp. 225–43.

5. See article by George McBride on "Land Tenure – Latin America" in *Encyclopedia of the Social Sciences*, 1950 edition, Vol. IX, pp. 118–27.

unscrupulous tradesmen, money lenders, lawyers and petty officials.

It should be emphasized that the *minifundio-latifundio* patterns are not independent, but are often closely interrelated. Large estates are surrounded by many small *ranchos, chacras, huertas, hijuelas* or *sitios,* drawing seasonal labor from them and in many ways contributing to the maintenance of the system. The *latifundios* exercise an influence far beyond their own boundaries, and they are frequently a limiting force on regional development. More importantly, perhaps, the system acts as a barrier to social mobility, participating citizenship and the emergence of a broad base for upgrading the quality of human effort, which is a prerequisite for dynamic development.

The Comunidad

The third major type of land holding in Latin America is the *comunidad,* far older in origin than the *hacienda* or the plantation. The Incas, Mayas and Aztecs all held land in collective fashion, and the survival of the system is today localized in areas of native Indian populations, mostly in the Andean areas. The number of Indians living on the plateaus and in the valleys of the Andean chain between northern Argentina and Ecuador has been estimated as between 5 and 6 million. The Indian *comunidad,* while being slowly eroded away, is a remarkably durable institution. Its base is the aggregation of extended families, who together have claim over a specific land area. The territory of the community is deemed non-transferable, but the proprietary rights of the several families are recognized and every individual is free to dispose of his land within the group. In modern times many communities have *de facto* subdivided and individualized their land holdings, but in most there is a periodic reallocation of land among members. Much of the work is performed collectively on an exchange basis. Sociologists and anthropologists have given considerable attention to the Indian *comunidades* and have viewed them as heirs to the Inca *ayllus.*[6]

6. See George M. McBride, *Agrarian Indian Communities of Highland Bolivia,* Research Series No. 5, American Geographical Society, New York, 1921; also International Labour Office, *Conditions of Life and Work of Indigenous Populations of Latin American Countries,* Geneva, 1959.

A throwback to the *comunidades* is the Mexican *ejido,* product of the revolutionary land reform. Half the farmers in Mexico today are *ejidatarios.* Although the *ejido* system is much more closely connected with the social and economic mainstream of the country than are the geographically and culturally isolated *comunidades* of Peru, Bolivia or Ecuador, it suffers from very much the same economic ills. These communal arrangements, while embodying the seeds of cooperative economics, are excessively rigid and inhibit developmental forces. Members of the Andean communities are not able to obtain credit. There are no incentives for talented or ambitious individuals, and the system is not conducive to the emergence of effective leaders or group action in behalf of greater productivity. Capital investment by individuals is not encouraged. Thus the system in its present form represents a stagnant type of agriculture. Its main justification is on sociological grounds. For that part of the agricultural population which cannot be absorbed by the commercial farming sector or by urban occupations it offers perhaps a more secure and satisfactory way of life than that of the *colonos* or *peones.*

There has been considerable speculation about the possibilities of transforming the *comunidades* into modern cooperatives or true collectives, but apart from a few isolated cases, this has never been attempted on any meaningful scale. Several of the most recent land reform proposals (notably in Peru and Ecuador) contemplate such a transformation. While the obstacles are formidable the basic idea is intellectually attractive and challenging. Why wait until small independent owners can be organized into cooperatives, when the basic cultural framework may permit skipping such an intermediate stage? Yet it seems a long way from the communal *fiestas* to the bookkeeping system of a modern cooperative.

The Colono System

The last major feature of the Latin American tenure system worth recording here is the pattern of agricultural labor. In a region where the majority of farm people are not owners of land, the systems of farm labor have a decisive influence on productivity and levels of living. In spite of its importance, this is a greatly neglected field. The available information on farm labor, and its multiple combination with sharecropping and tenancy, is conspicuously deficient.

In general, only a small fraction of workers in the countries are paid on a cash basis. Most have the status of tenant laborers, a typical arrangement that assumes many names and variants throughout Latin America. This is known as the *colono* system, in which the worker is paid in the temporary or traditional usufruct of a parcel of land and certain other privileges. In return, the *colono* must serve a specified number of days on the estate and fulfill other customary obligations, such as making available members of his family for certain tasks in the field or in the owner's household. This system is often combined with sharecropping or with tenancy on a cash rent basis. Most of the resident labor force on the *hacienda* is made up of *colonos*. They have different names in different countries: *yanaconas* in Peru, *inquilinos* in Chile, *huasipungos* in Ecuador, or *conuqueros* in Venezuela. Basically, all these represent similar arrangements.[7]

The *colono* pattern is regarded as inefficient and as a poor base for economic development. The duality of the structure with its quasi-security aspects is not conducive to production incentives for the *colonos*, thus compounding the debilitating effects of landlord absenteeism.

In countries that have introduced land reforms the *colonos* were the first and most important beneficiaries of the programs. In Bolivia, for instance, the major immediate effect of the reform was to confirm the possession of the tenant workers who have been occupying and working small plots on the *haciendas*.

In contrast with other world areas, tenancy in its pure form does not loom large in the agrarian structure of Latin America. Important exceptions are Argentina and Uruguay. In Argentina, commercial tenancy is numerically more important than owner operation. In Uruguay, about one-third of the land in farms is managed by tenants. In the rest of the countries the degree of tenancy is relatively low.[8] Contracts are generally of very short

7. For a good account of the *colono* pattern and its variants, see Sam Schulman, "The Colono System in Latin America," *Rural Sociology*, Vol. 20, No. 1, March 1955, pp. 34–40. See also International Labour Office, *Los agricultores sin tierras en América Latina*, Geneva, 1957.

8. João Gonçalves de Souza, "Aspects of Land Tenure Problems in Latin America," *Rural Sociology*, Vol. 25, No. 1, March 1960, pp. 36–37.

duration, and are verbal more often than not. Few of the norms of equitable and forward-looking tenancy arrangements are observed.

This review of the agrarian structure, brief and sketchy though it is, clearly shows the inadequacy of tenure institutions throughout the region. Units of production are either too large or too small, ownership and occupancy are often precarious, the communities are tradition-bound and inflexible, farm labor conditions are not many steps removed from serfdom, land as a resource does not freely exchange hands but is hoarded and unavailable to the small cultivator. There is no "tenure ladder" in the sense that a landless person could gradually work his way into the ownership class. Owners and non-owners of land are frequently separated by strict racial and cultural class barriers. The system reinforces the status quo and confers power upon those with inherited position and wealth. Farm investment is low, demand for consumer goods restricted, and large segments of the population are held at the margin of the economic mainstream in the countries. Political democracy and social mobility are greatly circumscribed. For brevity and simplicity the picture described is based only on land tenure conditions. If one were to superimpose the effects of the other institutional factors – which in addition to what may be called "access to land" include access to capital and access to markets, the tax structure, education, local government and other related aspects – the situation would appear even darker.[9]

RECENT ATTEMPTS AT REFORMS

Historically, the pressure for land tenure reforms has been motivated mainly by social justice and equity considerations. The implicit and explicit aim of all land reforms in the region has been

9. Agriculture is lagging behind other sectors in Latin America. In spite of good advances in some areas and with respect to some products, its overall growth barely keeps pace with population. During the decade 1950–60 population increased at an average rate of 2.5 per cent per year, while the rate of growth for agricultural production was 3 per cent per year.

Of course, not all the ills of Latin American agriculture can be ascribed to land tenure conditions. Many other factors are also at work. But the land systems are undoubtedly among the fundamental causes of the slow rate of growth in agriculture.

the substitution of the *latifundio-minifundio-colono* pattern by one based on a much greater amount of owner cultivation or by communally owned larger units in which the cultivator has security and increased status. In societies where the possession of land means wealth, security and status, one can easily understand the appeal of the cry: "Land to the tiller!" In what follows, an attempt will be made to review in capsule fashion some of the important land reforms that had been started in Latin countries by 1960.

Mexico

The first and earliest of land reforms in Latin America was the Mexican one. It has fundamentally altered the land tenure situation in that country. The history of the Mexican land reform, which has been a major element in the revolution, is long and complex. Much has been written about it and after almost four decades it still forms the subject of considerable controversy.[10] How relevant the Mexican experience is for other countries is debatable. It can be argued that the situation a generation ago was quite different from that prevailing today and that the prolonged revolutionary struggles which formed the matrix for the land reform as well as the *ejido*[11] which emerged were unique. Yet the Mexican experience is the only one which provides us with a long enough perspective to evaluate the effect of fundamental tenure changes on development.

The main outlines of the new land policy were written into the Mexican constitution of 1917. The key provision, in Article 27, revolves around the government's right to expropriate private

10. The following are selections from the enormous literature on the Mexican land reform: Nathan L. Whetten, *Rural Mexico,* University of Chicago Press, Chicago, 1948; Frank Tannenbaum, *Mexico – The Struggle for Peace and Bread,* Alfred Knopf, New York, 1951; Ramón Fernández y Fernández, "La reforma agraria mexicana," *El Trimestre Económico,* Vol. 24, No. 94, 1957; Jesús Silva Herzog, *El agrarismo mexicano y la reforma agraria,* Fondo de Cultura Económica, Mexico, 1959; Clarence Senior, *Land Reform and Democracy,* University of Florida Press, Gainesville, 1958.

11. The *ejido* is a system of communal tenure in which lands are held as the property of a town or village either for collective use or for distribution among the *ejidatarios* for cultivation in small plots to which each individual has a right of occupancy and usufruct. *Ejido* lands cannot be sold or mortgaged.

property and the methods for land distribution. The unusual feature of the Mexican reform is, of course, the tenure of the new units. The goal here was a special form of communal tenure, called the *ejido,* which was modeled on the ancient native communities whose land was usurped by the *hacienda.* The transformation of the *hacienda* into *ejidos* was a long, awkward and often bloody process. A recent study by James Maddox summarizes this process admirably:

> The expropriation of private property to turn it over to people who only a few years before had had a status hardly different from that of slaves, struck deep, hard blows at the very heart of the value systems . . . Almost any schoolboy can look back over what happened and see countless errors of judgment, an almost total lack of forward planning, inequities in the application of the law, and private gain and personal greed going unchecked even though they were contrary to the spirit and letter of the law and the professed aims of the Revolution. Civil strife, bloodshed, confiscation of private property, greed and errors in its redistribution, were all a part of the process of redistributing the land. . . . [The history of the period suggests that] the old, landed aristocracy . . . wasn't willing to give an inch in the direction of wider opportunities for the agricultural *peones.* . . . the end of the fighting war did not resolve the basic conflict. . . . It was a hard, and often bloody, struggle all through the twenties and early thirties. Landlords were recalcitrant; the *peones* and their representatives were often hoodwinked; sometimes the *peones* were patient, but generally they were adamant that they receive land; laws were not clear, and were constantly being changed; the courts often sided with the landowners almost regardless of how the laws were drafted. The struggle shifted from battlefields to government offices and courtrooms. Two systems of social values were locked in a death struggle.[12]

In spite of the revolutionary backing for the reforms, the land distribution process started very slowly. As Table 2 shows, during the first eighteen years only 7.8 million hectares of land, about 6 per cent of all the land in farms, were distributed. It was President Cárdenas who carried out the major part of the distribution program. One-half of all the land distributed between 1916 and 1956 changed hands during the six years (1934–40) of his administration. The Ejidal Bank, as a special credit institution for

12. James G. Maddox, *Mexican Land Reform,* American Universities Field Staff, JGM-5-'57, New York, 1957.

TABLE 2

MEXICO: LAND DISTRIBUTION IN FOUR DECADES

Period	*Number of Hectares Distributed (thousands)* Total	Average per Year	*Number of Persons Receiving Land (thousands)* Total	Average per Year
1916–34	7,800	409	783	41
1935–40	17,900	2,982	815	136
1941–56	11,100	743	267	18
Total	36,800	920	1,865	47

Source: Adapted from James G. Maddox, *Mexican Land Reform,* American Universities Field Staff, JGM-5-'57, New York, 1957, p. 17.

ejidatarios, was also organized during the Cárdenas period. After his regime, the reform slowed down notably.

According to the 1950 census, there were 17,579 *ejidos* in the country representing a total of almost 39 million hectares of land and 1.4 million *ejidatarios.* The land in *ejidos* comprised about 27 per cent of all land in farms and about 44 per cent of the land in crops. Data from the 1950 census in Table 3 indicate the tenure

TABLE 3

MEXICO: TENURE STATUS OF FARM FAMILIES, 1950

Tenure Status	*Number of Farm Families (thousands)*	*Per Cent of Total*
Owner operators	1,262	26.5
Ejidatarios	1,393	29.2
Farm managers	84	1.7
Tenants, sharecroppers and other operators	18	0.4
Landless farm workers	2,010	42.2
Total	4,767	100.0

Source: Documentación Básica, República de México, Documento IP-13, Segundo Seminario de la FAO Sobre Problemas de la Tierra, Montevideo, 1959 (mimeographed).

status of Mexican farmers and the importance of the reforms. It can be observed that over half of Mexican farm families have a stake in the land.

The process of breaking up large holdings is still going on. About 23 per cent of the holdings are still in units of more than 200 hectares. Quite similarly to the structure of many other countries which have not undergone reforms, 10,000 farms in the private sector (representing less than 1 per cent of all farms) occupy 76 per cent of the total private acreage. Moreover, as Maddox points out, there is considerable evidence that in recent years private property in farm lands has been increasing more rapidly than the *ejido* system of tenure. For instance, whereas in 1940, soon after the spurt of land distribution by the Cárdenas administration, 47.4 per cent of the nation's cropland was in *ejidos*, by 1950 the proportion had fallen to 44.1 per cent.

All writers agree that the main politico-social objective of the reform – the elimination of the *latifundios* and the institutions they maintained – was accomplished. It is also generally acknowledged that the reform has given a tremendous boost to the consolidation of stable and representative government, to a cultural renaissance and, indirectly, to the extraordinarily rapid rate of economic development during the forties and fifties. This is what Maddox says:

> . . . most of the available evidence points toward the conclusion that Mexico has made giant strides in becoming a united nation, in speeding up economic, social, and political development, and in raising the levels of living of at least 95 per cent of her people, *precisely because* of her Revolution. Moreover, land reform was the single most important ingredient of the Mexican Revolution, and it is quite probable that its other component parts, such as a national program of public education, the building of a national highway system, the fostering of an organized labor movement, and heavy emphasis on industrializing the country, would not have gone forward with anything like the speed that they have, if there had not been a redistribution of the land.

There is sharp disagreement, however, on the present and potential value of the *ejido* system and the future course for Mexican land policy. It is argued that the really significant advances have been made in the private sector of agriculture, especially in newly developed areas, and that the *ejido,* while it once fulfilled a legitimate social need, is no longer a proper vehicle for economic development, the big issue of the day. It is felt that a "reform of the reform" is needed to bring the agrarian structure in line with the dynamic requirements of technical progress.[13] At the same time the old line *agraristas* assert that, on the contrary, a strengthening of the *ejidos* is in order and that their poor economic performance is not so much a result of basic weakness of the system as lack of outside help, such as credit, marketing and other essential services. They also point out that recent more conservative governments have paid much more attention to the private sector and to nonagricultural matters than to the *ejidos.*

Even though all large holdings have not been broken up, and private property has increased more rapidly in recent years than *ejido* holdings, the fact remains that Mexico has had a significant revolution in her system of land tenure. Land reform has not only made sweeping changes in the organization and functioning of the agricultural segment of the economy, but it has been the "catalyst" of a large chain of complex socio-economic movements which have pushed forward the country's over-all development.

Bolivia

After Mexico it is the Bolivian land reform that has been in operation for the longest period of time. The Bolivian law was issued in August 1953. It was also the outcome of violent revolution and has not been subject to constitutional processes. Richard Patch, a careful student of Bolivian social change since 1952, reports that in the early months after the revolution the national government did not regard land reform as a major issue and contemplated to revive some older legislation which put certain restrictions on *hacienda* owners. It was a genuine peasant uprising, started in the Cochabamba area where *campesinos* drove landowners off their estates, that decided the government on a more

13. The most articulate and thoughtful critic of the present structure is Ing. Ramón Fernández y Fernández. See his *Propiedad privada versus ejidos,* Escuela Nacional de Agricultura, Mexico, 1954.

13a. Richard W. Patch, "Bolivia: U. S. Assistance in a Revolutionary Setting," in Council on Foreign Relations, *Social Change in Latin America Today,* Harper & Brothers, New York, 1960, pp. 108–76.

drastic course of action.[13a] President Paz Estenssoro then created a committee on agrarian reform which was given 120 days to study the agrarian problems and produce a law, or more precisely a decree. In the screening of the various projects the Bolivian Central Labor Union, an important political force within the ruling MNR Party, had a prominent part.

The fundamental objectives mentioned in the preamble of the decree are: (1) redistribution of land that does not perform a "social function"; (2) development of Indian communities; (3) reform of agricultural labor relations; (4) promotion of agricultural development; (5) conservation of natural resources; (6) stimulation of internal migration. Article 30 declares that *latifundios* are abolished, while Article 35 specifically exempts from expropriation large farms in which the owner has made substantial capital investments, uses modern methods and works his own land personally. According to Article 153 expropriated landlords are to be given compensation in the form of 25-year agrarian bonds. The value of the land was fixed on the basis of current tax assessment (subsequently it was raised to five times the basic tax value). Article 160 provides that the beneficiaries are to pay for land grants exactly on the same terms as the payment to landlords.[14]

The main problem the law was designed to remedy was the extreme land concentration. The pre-reform figures of 1950 are given in Table 4. In the perspective of eight years it is now possible to make a tentative evaluation of the reforms. A good study has been made by Heath[15] and some figures have been released by the National Agrarian Reform Service. With the general disorganization after the revolution and the lack of personnel and administration, the reform got off to a very slow start. However, it began to pick up speed in 1960. Up to the end of 1960 some 59,000 heads of families had received land grants (23,000 in 1960 alone). It has been reported that if all the pending applications in La Paz and in the various regional offices are finally processed, an additional

14. For the background of the reform see Edmundo Flores, "Land Reform in Bolivia," *Land Economics*, Vol. 30, No. 2, May 1954, pp. 112–24.

15. Dwight B. Heath, "Land Reform in Bolivia," *Inter-American Economic Affairs*, Vol. 12, No. 4, 1959, pp. 3–27.

TABLE 4

BOLIVIA: DISTRIBUTION OF FARMS AND FARM LAND BY SIZE OF UNIT, 1950 (PRIOR TO LAND REFORM)

Size of Farms (hectares)	Number of Farms		Number of Hectares	
	(Thousands)	Per Cent	(Thousands)	Per Cent
0–20	66	78	216	1
20–100	8	9	326	1
100–1,000	6	7	2,102	6
Over 1,000	5	6	30,099	92
Total	85	100	32,743	100

Source: Adapted from Documentación Básica, Bolivia, Documento IP–2, Segundo Seminario de la FAO Sobre Problemas de la Tierra, Montevideo, 1959 (mimeographed).

47,000 families will have received land titles. It is not known what percentage of the potential number of beneficiaries these figures represent. Estimates of the total number of eligible families range all the way from 100,000 to over 200,000. Should the actual number be closer to the lower estimate, the land distribution process may be nearing its end.

There is no reliable information on the area of land redistributed. The officially reported figure of 4.2 million hectares distributed or in process of distribution by the end of 1960 (which represents about 13 per cent of all the land in farms) includes land still in the hands of the landlords.

Almost no compensation for expropriation has been made to former landlords. In the meantime most of their claim as originally fixed has been wiped out by the rampant inflation. Beneficiaries have not yet been asked to pay for their new holdings, but they should have little difficulty in doing so as the level of legal payments has depreciated to an insignificant fraction of their original value.

Heath reports that after five years of reforms few of the basic objectives stated in the law were realized. All observers describe the immediate aftermath of the reform as a period of chaos and lawlessness. Armed peasants occupied lands, chased away many owners and destroyed a considerable amount of capital investments including livestock. The government did not have the technical, financial and administrative resources to organize the reform in a systematic way, much less to give the new owners the complementary services they so badly needed. In general, the first five years of the reform were characterized by extreme economic disorganization, rampant inflation and political struggles. There was also a great deal of insecurity about the peasants' rights. Small wonder that farm production fell, or at least that the marketable surplus decreased considerably. According to figures of the U.S.-ICA Operations Mission, the index of agricultural production fell by almost one-third by 1954–55 and has not yet fully recovered the pre-reform level. It is only during the last year or so that a substantial improvement in production is noticeable, but much of the increase in cultivated acreage and produce comes from relatively new areas, such as the *yungas* and the department of Santa Cruz, which have been least affected by the land reform. Apparently no great change has occurred in the income of the cultivators. It is likely that they have maintained or slightly bettered their position as the burdens of food shortages and inflation have fallen on urban groups.

The Bolivian land reform has thus far lacked even a minimal technical basis. Hence there is a danger that the possible economic benefit will not be realized or will be unduly postponed. Yet the feudal structure, which in Bolivia was particularly oppressive, is abolished, and the Indian is in process of "liberation." The country has found a national unity and purpose. Education has received a great impetus; since the land reform, the number of schools and teachers has doubled. Colonization programs for the tropical areas are being planned. As the Bolivian *altiplano* presents a meager resource base, no amount of land distribution will solve the problem of the *minifundios*. Therefore, land settlement of new areas and land reform in the highlands must be parallel and simultaneous programs.

Guatemala

Brief mention should be made of the much debated and abortive land reform of Guatemala. The land tenure and farm labor situation in Guatemala is among the least satisfactory in Latin

America. In 1952 the Arbenz government initiated a comprehensive land reform program. For all the furor it produced, Decree 900, which had its roots in the constitution of 1945, is a remarkably mild and a fairly sound piece of legislation.

It provides for the expropriation and redistribution of uncultivated or fallow lands above a basic limit. It specifically exempts intensively cultivated farms, including those growing plantation crops. (In 1950 the large holdings of over 1,000 hectares had only 5 per cent of their land under cultivation.) However, absentee-owned or tenanted properties were to be redistributed. Compensation was offered in the form of agrarian reform bonds maturing in twenty-five years. The basis of the assessment was to be the declared tax value. An additional provision in the law decrees the granting of state lands in permanent usufruct to individuals or to cooperatives. (This provision is in line with the Guatemala constitution, according to which state lands cannot be permanently alienated.)

It appears that, in spite of deficient and confused administrative machinery, the land distribution made considerable advance in a little more than a year. Lands of 107 state farms taken over from German owners during World War II and covering over 300,000 hectares were subdivided. Sixty-one of these were divided among 7,800 small farmers and 46 were organized into cooperatives. In addition, 254 private farms covering some 200,000 hectares were expropriated. The most controversial move of the government was the expropriation of 160,000 hectares of uncultivated land from the United Fruit Company. The company argued that it needed these lands as banana growing reserves for rotation to combat diseases. It also protested against the low valuation. The government contended that the company's land reserves on the Atlantic coast alone were over twenty times the actually cultivated banana acreage.[16] What the facts are in this and other subsequent controversies would require careful research. One thing is certain: the reform measures ran into powerful opposition. They touched sensitive issues and became embroiled in doctrinaire struggles. There is no reliable information on how much land

16. A. Fuentes-Mohr, "Land Settlement and Agrarian Reform in Guatemala," *International Journal of Agrarian Affairs,* Oxford University Press, London, Vol. 2, No. 1, Jan. 1955, pp. 26–36.

changed hands. According to one writer, approximately 100,000 families received (or occupied) some land under the program.[17] At the same time very few actual titles were given out. The National Agrarian Credit Bank, whose main task was to support the agrarian reform, was established in 1953.

The land reform was washed away in the political and military events of 1954. Rightly or wrongly, it is widely believed in Latin America that opposition to the land reform by the United Fruit Company and the United States government was an important factor in the downfall of the Arbenz government. In any event, Decree 900 was revoked in 1954 and replaced by other bills which carry no effective provisions for change in the agrarian structure. Since that time, a modest amount of planned colonization has taken place with the help of the U. S. Point Four program. In six years about 4,000 families have been settled on commercial-sized farms, some 4,200 additional families have received suburban *micro-parcelas* averaging 2.5 hectares, and 12,000 members of Indian communities have been given rights to land in the amount of 5.3 hectares per family.

Cuba

An intelligent and meaningful discussion of the Cuban land reform is uncommonly difficult. There is not much factual information, the situation is fluid, and it is much too early to appreciate what has been done with what results. Yet no discussion of land reform in Latin America would be complete without some account of the Cuban phenomenon, which, after all, has spotlighted the problem most strongly.

The land problems of Cuba, and the measures adopted for their solution, differ considerably from the Mexico-Bolivia pattern. Cuba has enjoyed a relatively high level of living among Latin American countries, though very unequally distributed, to be sure, especially in farming. Its agriculture is dominated by monoculture of sugar, an export crop.

At the time of the revolution the land situation in Cuba was characterized by extremely poor utilization of land and human resources. Only about one-half of the farm land was cultivated.

17. Oscar René Cruz, "La reforma agraria de Guatemala," *Revista de Economía,* December 1958, pp. 326–28.

TABLE 5

CUBA: DISTRIBUTION OF FARMS AND FARM LAND BY SIZE OF UNIT, 1946

	Number of Farms		*Number of Hectares*	
Farm Size (hectares)	*Thousands*	*Per Cent*	*Thousands*	*Per Cent*
0–25	111	69.6	1,022	11.2
25–100	36	22.5	1,608	17.7
100–1,000	12	7.4	3,186	35.0
Over 1,000	1	.5	3,261	36.1
Total	160	100.0	9,077	100.0

Source: Adapted from Documentación Básica, República de Cuba, Documento IP–7, Segundo Seminario de la FAO Sobre Problemas de la Tierra, Montevideo, 1959 (mimeographed).

Cuba imported an enormous amount of food, in the value of almost $100 million annually, and farm labor suffered from chronic underemployment. The distribution of holdings in 1946 is given in Table 5. The land concentration was aggravated by the fact that the sugar plantations, in addition to owning about 50 per cent of the cultivable land, were renting 800,000 hectares, thereby controlling almost three-fourths of the cultivable area of the country. This monopoly situation with regard to land is without parallel in the whole region. Another special feature of the Cuban land tenure complex was the wide extent of foreign ownership.

As is well known, land reform was one of the main platforms of the Cuban revolution. As promulgated in May 1959, the land reform law provides for the establishment of maximum limits for land holdings (393 hectares), and for the establishment of a "vital minimum" for a farm family in order to permit an acceptable level of living. The basic minimum is 26.8 hectares of non-irrigated productive land, distant from urban centers.[18]

Lands subject to expropriation are to be paid for in bonds over twenty years with interest at 4.5 per cent. Up to the vital minimum, land grants are to be made free of charge; above that the

18. For an analysis of the land reform law see Marco Antonio Durán, "La reforma agraria cubana," *El Trimestre Económico,* Vol. 27, No. 107, July–Sept. 1960, pp. 410–69. (The article includes the full text of the law.)

new owners are to pay for the land under favorable terms. First priority in redistribution is to be given to small tenants, sharecroppers and occupants and second priority to landless workers.

A departure from previous reforms is the preoccupation with production organization. The organization of cooperatives, especially in sugar cane areas, is greatly emphasized, and restrictions are placed upon the owners of new units in behalf of rational farming.

It is estimated that 7 million hectares, or 75 per cent of the total farming area, is subject to the land reform. Approximately 69,000 small farmers are eligible to receive land under the vital minimum provision. Between 2½ and 3 million hectares would be distributed free of charge.

The administrative organization that has emerged for carrying out the law is interesting. In sharp contrast with the generally weak, underfinanced and understaffed organizations of other countries (such as the Departamento Agrario in Mexico or the Ministerio de Asuntos Campesinos in Bolivia), the revolutionary government in Cuba has created a strong, autonomous body called the National Institute for Land Reform (Instituto Nacional de Reforma Agraria, or INRA). INRA has been gradually endowed with vast powers; since its creation it has absorbed among other things the agricultural credit functions of the National Development Bank for Agriculture and Industry (BANFAIC) and, more recently, the tasks of the Ministry of Agriculture. Thus, INRA has developed into a super agency which along with administering land reform is responsible for the planning and direction of all farm policy.[19]

While the large holdings were rapidly expropriated or confiscated, the distribution process started very slowly. By the end of the first year of the reform, fewer than 1,800 titles had been issued to small cultivators. By the end of October 1960 the number of small land grants issued had been stepped up to 20,000, and by February 1961 to 30,000.

It is believed that by the end of 1960 all lands subject to ex-

19. A good analysis of the initial steps taken under the Cuban land reform is contained in Food and Agriculture Organization of the United Nations (FAO), *Draft Report of the FAO Regional Land Reform Team for Latin America,* Rome, July 1960 (mimeographed).

propriation had already been taken over by INRA or were in process of nationalization. The area thus affected is estimated as a little over 4 million hectares. This constitutes approximately one-half the total area which landowners reported in compliance with the land reform law. The great bulk of the acreage taken over by the government has not been distributed but is being managed by INRA through its own officials or by army personnel. This applies especially to the livestock estates. In the sugar areas so-called cooperatives have been formed, which actually represent the old sugar estates under new management. It was reported that 600 to 700 sugar cooperatives were functioning at the end of 1960 with an average of 1,300 to 1,500 hectares each. Little is known of the way these farms are operated, nor is it known to what extent these cooperatives are intended eventually to be under self-management. Only one case has been reported in which legal title was granted to a sugar cooperative.

By the end of 1960 the outlines of future policy were beginning to emerge. It seems that there will be three major sectors of Cuban agriculture:

1. About one-half the agricultural land will belong to the private sector with individual holdings of up to about 40 hectares each (with somewhat more for livestock farms).

2. The second sector will include the sugar cooperatives mentioned above. These are expected to develop into an intermediate type of tenure with some private and some public elements.

3. Finally, there is now a plan to establish very large state farms in the remaining areas. These would cover several thousand hectares each and would be administered directly by INRA.

There is very scarce information on payment for land. According to INRA, by the end of 1960, bonds in the value of 5½ million dollars had been issued and cash payments amounting to 1¼ million dollars made. It is widely believed, however, that much of the land was confiscated outright.

Little is known about the immediate income and production effects of the reforms. Because of the rapid political and economic changes in Cuba, it is well-nigh impossible to sort out what can and what cannot be attributed to the reforms themselves. Production in 1959–60 did not seem to suffer. There is contradictory opinion concerning the level of living of the beneficiaries. While the government seems to have held wages on the sugar farms below the average of the private sector, the purchasing power of the farm workers may have been maintained through the establishment of government stores (*tiendas del pueblo*) which sell food and household products at low prices. On the other hand, a large portion of wages is issued in scrip spendable only at these stores where the assortment of available goods may be quite limited.

The course of the Cuban land reform will be interesting to watch. It seems a pity that this experiment has been so intimately mixed up with and overshadowed by broader political and ideological issues, and indeed by the Cold War. The sorting out of the various facets of the Cuban land situation will be a challenging task for social scientists for many years to come.

It is already clear that the land reform has shifted away from the original aims of the revolution. The early revolutionary platforms and declarations of Fidel Castro on land reform prior to the take-over in 1959 differed significantly from the law itself and from the subsequent policy of implementation. A careful analyst of the Cuban scene, Theodore Draper, points out that all pre-1959 revolutionary programs promised grants of land to small farmers with clear titles and just compensation to former owners.[19a] Cooperatives occupied only a relatively minor role in the platform and were treated in the traditional sense, based on services for independent landowners. The collectivization and state farm ideas were apparently developed later, after the take-over. Draper concludes that the Cuban revolution was not a genuine peasant revolt as in Mexico and Bolivia, but essentially a middle class one which turned against the middle class. In Bolivia the revolution permitted the *campesinos* to take over lands; in Cuba it was the government or the army which took the land over for them and is managing it in their behalf.

Venezuela

The Venezuelan land reform is the most recent of the big programs, having been promulgated in March 1960. It is an interesting and in many respects unique case. While akin to other comprehensive agrarian movements, in that the Venezuelan basic law

19a. Theodore Draper, "Castro's Cuba," *Encounter*, Vol. XVI, No. 3, March 1961, pp. 6–23.

is also the outgrowth of a revolution, its history does not follow the Mexican, Bolivian or Guatemalan pattern. The party of Rómulo Betancourt campaigned actively upon the issue of land reform. When it came into power, the new president appointed a non-partisan commission representing prominent political figures and private individuals of all shades of opinion. It organized itself into four subcommittees, charged respectively with legal, economic, social and agro-technical aspects. The subcommittees did a good deal of research and held hearings to get outside opinions. Most of the debates which normally accompany the drafting of important laws in legislative bodies took place within the commission. The result was a law that was approved by the Venezuelan congress with few modifications. The full texts of the deliberations of the four subcommissions have been published and they make for very interesting reading.[20]

Apart from the orderly manner in which the preliminary study was set up and the legal machinery established, the Venezuelan law is notable for its broad coverage, as it deals not only with problems of land tenure but also with other aspects of a comprehensive agricultural policy. The key provisions of the law established the concept of "social function of landed property." Under this concept, only three kinds of land are subject to expropriation: uncultivated lands; farms worked indirectly through renters, sharecroppers and other intermediaries; and lands suitable for cultivation but devoted to natural pasture for extensive livestock raising. A further provision states that private lands can only be expropriated if no publicly owned properties are available in the same area. The law also fixes the absolute size limits below which private land cannot be expropriated. However, in certain cases of serious pressure, land can be expropriated without regard to size and land use criteria.

The lands taken over are to be paid for in cash up to the value of $30,000; above this value, the payment is to be part in cash and part in bonds. Payment is to be made at current market value. High priority in the selection of new settlers is given to those actually cultivating the lands subject to redistribution. The sales price to new owners is made up of the cost of purchase plus im-

20. Venezuela, Ministerio de Agricultura y Cría, Comisión de Reforma Agraria, *Reforma agraria,* Vols. I–IV, Caracas, 1959.

provements and the payment can be extended over a period of twenty to thirty years. In some cases land can be distributed free of charge.

In addition to these basic measures, the law contains provisions for the imposition of graduated land taxes, in order to force the owners of the large farms to cultivate their properties more intensively or to sell them. Further articles deal with farm credit, marketing, extension services, cooperatives, land development and other supplementary measures.

Approximately 2,500 large farms exceed the legal limits and therefore could technically be expropriated. These farms include over 15 million hectares, which is over half of all the land in farms.

According to announced objectives, the Venezuelan land reform is intended to benefit approximately 300,000 rural families within the next ten years. This figure would seem to include practically all the "landless" families in Venezuela. According to 1956 data, of the approximately 400,000 farms in Venezuela a little over 100,000 are operated by tenants and sharecroppers, while almost one-half of all the units – little less than 200,000 – are worked under miscellaneous and not defined types of tenure. If it is assumed that most of these latter farms represent illegal occupants or squatters, the job involves giving titles *in situ* and resettlement in the proportion of about 2 to 1.

In a recent speech, the Minister of Agriculture declared that once the reform took hold, through these two programs of confirming squatters' rights and resettling tenants and sharecroppers, land grants would be made to 30,000–40,000 families annually. This would indeed be a most impressive achievement.

Table 6 shows the distribution of holdings with which the reform will have to deal. These data assume more significance when one notes that according to the agricultural survey of 1956 only one-fourth of all farms were owner-operated, and that less than 10 per cent of the agricultural land was in crops. Farms over 1,000 hectares had only 3.7 per cent in crops.

Another unusual feature of the Venezuelan land reform is the extraordinary amount of governmental appropriations available to carry out the law. The National Agrarian Institute, which up to 1959 was in charge of all the colonization programs, has become the executive agency for the new land reform program. Apart

TABLE 6

VENEZUELA: DISTRIBUTION OF FARMS AND FARM LAND BY SIZE OF UNIT, 1956

Size Group (hectares)	Number of Farms		Number of Hectares	
	Thousands	*Per Cent*	*Thousands*	*Per Cent*
0–20	350	88.0	1,623	5.4
20–100	27	7.0	1,340	4.6
100–1,000	14	3.4	4,589	16.0
Over 1,000	7	1.6	22,038	74.0
Total	398	100.0	29,590	100.0

Source: Encuesta Agropecuaria Nacional de 1956. Adapted from Documentación Básica de Venezuela, Documento IP–18, Segundo Seminario de la FAO Sobre Problemas de la Tierra, Montevideo, 1959 (mimeographed).

from its initial capital of 100 million bolivars (about $30 million) and the value of public lands assigned to it, the Institute had a budget of 104 million bolivars for the fiscal year 1959–60 and 150 million for 1960–61. This does not include the amount that is being authorized for the issuance of land bonds or the amount available for farm credit through the Agricultural Bank in support of the land reform. It is obvious that with financing of this magnitude much can be accomplished even under the relatively mild provisions of the law. Human and organizational resources are likely to be more wanting than monetary resources.

Although it is much too early to be able to evaluate the Venezuelan land reform, it is clear that the pace of land settlement has been considerably stepped-up during the first year of the program. During the ten-year period prior to the land reform the colonization agencies managed to settle approximately 10,000 families (one-half of them in 1959). During the first six months of the new reforms (between April and September 1960) the Institute had already granted over 13,000 titles.[21] It appears that the first expropriations were made on land confiscated from supporters of the previous regime under special emergency legislation. It also

21. Venezuela, Instituto Agrario Nacional, *Informes mensuales,* Caracas, 1960.

appears that a number of large landowners are anxious to sell their estates to the Institute at favorable market prices.

The Venezuelan reform is something of a test case. Should it be possible for the country to solve its basic land problems by peaceful and constitutional means, this would undoubtedly provide an example to a number of countries. The cumulative effect of the measures supporting land distribution, such as credit, land development and marketing, will also be an interesting test of what the Christian Democratic Minister of Agriculture, Dr. Victor Giménez, likes to call "the integrated approach to land reform."[22]

COLONIZATION SCHEMES

The foregoing account highlights the programs of those countries which have embarked on large and comprehensive land reforms. A number of other countries have for some years carried out planned land settlement programs. While the announced aim of these settlement or "colonization" projects is similar to those of wider and more drastic tenure reforms — that is, the creation of a large number of owner cultivators with medium-sized properties and adequate family incomes — their achievements have been limited.

Land settlement programs have been of two types. One involves the opening up of new or virgin lands or the creation of new settlement opportunities through large-scale irrigation, drainage, forestation and other land development measures. Such settlement is normally on public land. The other type includes the purchase, development and subdivision of privately owned farms in the already cultivated or "old" areas. Both programs are strictly limited by the amount of money available for land purchase and development.

In most cases, land settlement programs in Latin America can be regarded as little more than pilot schemes. This should not detract from their value. Indeed, these programs and the accumulated knowledge of the institutions which plan and execute them represent a most significant experience on which more comprehensive land reforms could draw in this difficult field.

While practically all the countries have some sort of land settle-

22. Victor Giménez Landínez, *Reforma agraria integral en Venezuela*, Mexico, August 1960.

ment policies and programs, the most notable are the activities in Uruguay, Chile, Colombia, Venezuela and Ecuador. The customary form of organization for land settlement is a semi-autonomous body created especially for the purpose. In Uruguay, for instance, a National Institute of Colonization was established in 1948. The basic law which created the Institute gives the following main objective: "To promote the rational subdivision of the land and its adequate utilization, in order to achieve the growth and improvement of agricultural production and the settlement and welfare of the rural worker." The main task of the Institute has been the purchase and redistribution of inadequately utilized large farms. Because of meager appropriations, in twelve years only about 1,300 new units have been established. However, the new settlements cover an area of 225,000 hectares and as they are being intensively cultivated with horticultural and industrial crops they are making an important contribution to agricultural output. The Institute has acquired an additional 210,000 hectares which it has not yet been able to distribute.

In Chile the instrument of land settlement is the Caja de Colonización, whose basic legislation was created as far back as 1928, although in its modern form it has operated only since 1935. As is true of its sister agency in Uruguay, the Caja's orientation and legal equipment are on the whole well conceived and workable. But the noble aims which brought the Caja into being have been frustrated by the well-known Chilean inflation, or perhaps more precisely, by the unwillingness of subsequent governments to put the Caja's appropriations and operations on a hard-money basis. In retrospect it can be seen that lack of effective pressure by the potential beneficiaries allowed the Caja to die a slow death. The result is that in almost twenty-six years new farms have been set up to the benefit of only some 3,300 families, many of whom were not bona fide landless cultivators.

Recently the Caja was given a new lease on life by a series of decrees which readjusted its finances and assigned to it for distribution the lands of a number of large government-owned farms of about 300,000 hectares. In addition, between the lands already held by the Caja and other public lands likely to be assigned to it, another one million hectares will soon be available for redistribution. (Half a million of this represents unimproved pasture land in the southernmost province of Magallanes where the Caja is assigning roughly 3,000 hectares per family unit.) While thus the rate of land settlement is likely to be accelerated considerably, it appears doubtful that under the existing circumstances the Caja can make significant improvements in the position of Chile's over 200,000 landless rural families.[23]

A National Colonization Institute was recently established in Ecuador. It has suffered from political birth pains under changing administrations. Up to now it has concentrated its efforts on a single pilot project, which involves a little over 100 families. The first big project of the Ecuadorian Institute will be the subdivision of state farms. This program is now being studied with the help of the United Nations Special Fund. About 133,000 hectares are likely to be affected. As there are extensive government lands in Ecuador, it is hoped that the rhythm of land settlement can be stepped up greatly without the need of expropriation.

Brief mention should be made of the land settlement efforts of Venezuela, prior to the land reform. The outstanding fact about this program was its very high cost and the meagerness of the results achieved. Enormous investments were made in such things as roads, houses, machinery and irrigation, which considering the number of people benefited and alternative opportunities for social investment, seem extravagant and misdirected. The model villages created were designed for a level of living which far exceeded that prevailing in surrounding areas. Another point which is frequently criticized in the Venezuelan colonization is the paternalistic attitude adopted by the settlement agency (Instituto Agrario Nacional). Everything was being done for the settlers, and in many cases they were even given prolonged cash subsidies. No attempt was made to develop individual or community initia-

23. A revealing commentary on the difficulties facing land reform in Chile is the following remarkably candid extract from the Chilean government's official reply to a United Nations questionnaire: "Owing to the economic and political structure of the country, land reform in Chile is difficult to carry out. Landholders who would be affected by any action of an economic, political, administrative, legal or social nature will vigorously oppose its implementation, and their political and economic influence is very powerful . . ." United Nations, *Progress in Land Reform,* Department of Economic Affairs, New York, 1954, p. 43.

tive or to put the projects on a sound economic basis.[24] There is some evidence that the present administration is well aware of these past errors and that the new projects under the land reform law are being planned more realistically.

Land settlement agencies similar to the ones in Chile and Uruguay are also operating in a number of other countries, including Paraguay, Brazil, Peru and Colombia. Some of them have good programs, but their total impact on the land tenure problem has been small.

In Colombia, for instance, the Caja Agraria administers a settlement program on public lands, and is also subdividing some private holdings. For 1959–60 this involved only about 1,000 families, but more resources will become available in future years. In 1959 a special law ordered the investment of 10 per cent of all savings deposits in bonds of the Caja for purposes of land redistribution. The Development Loan Fund and the Export-Import Bank have concluded a loan agreement for $70 million, of which about $33 million has been earmarked to support land settlement programs. By the end of 1960, plans were under way to resettle 50,000 families in five years.

LAND TAXATION

Thus far we have dealt mainly with what may be called a "direct" attack on land tenure problems. There is a body of theory with a considerable following among economists which holds that land reforms could be brought about by indirect methods, thereby avoiding the large social costs of drastic programs and the injustices implicit in radical redistribution of resources. Foremost among these indirect approaches is land taxation. For this purpose, land taxation would assume a double role; in addition to fulfilling a legitimate fiscal function, a properly adjusted and graduated land tax would gradually force the owners of estates either to intensify cultivation or to dispose of part of their holdings.

24. For an exceptional self-evaluation of the Venezuelan colonization programs see Ministerio de Agricultura y Cría, *La colonización agraria en Venezuela 1830–1957* (Estudio efectuado por el MAC con la colaboración del IAN), Caracas, 1959.

The experience with land taxation in Latin America is not encouraging. Colombia is the best example. As in other Latin American countries, land taxes in Colombia are extremely light and in many ways favor the large operators who have non-agricultural investments. The standard rate is 0.4 per cent.

Although the International Bank for Reconstruction and Development is generally reluctant to touch the controversial problems of land tenure, one of the principal recommendations of its missions to Colombia in 1950 and 1956 was the imposition of a graduated land tax based on potential land use. The first of these missions recommended (in what became known as the Currie Report) a graduated land tax which called for a rate of 0.4 per cent for well-utilized lands and higher rates for poorly used lands.[25] The 1956 mission suggested assessing agricultural land based on optimum rather than current use and subjecting owners of speculative holdings to an income tax based on a presumed net return of between 3 and 5 per cent of the value of land and capital assets.[26]

In 1957 governmental Decree 290 made a variant of these ideas into law, providing an elaborate system of tax incentives and deterrents designed to improve land use practices. The key provision required owners and tenants with more than fifty hectares to cultivate part of their land at least once a year. The cultivation requirements varied with the type of land, according to a classification to be made by the Geographic Institute. Non-compliance was to be punished by a progressive land tax based on cadastral value. There was no attempt in this decree to expropriate unused or underused private land whose owners did not comply with the cultivation quotas. The key to this whole procedure was the rapid completion of the land classification. A special ownership and use survey based on a questionnaire was also necessary to put the law into effect.

As of this writing, the penalties prescribed by Decree 290 for

25. International Bank for Reconstruction and Development, *The Basis for a Development Program for Colombia,* Johns Hopkins Press, Baltimore, 1950, pp. 384–87.

26. Sir Herbert R. Stewart, *et al., The Agricultural Development of Colombia,* International Bank for Reconstruction and Development, Washington, 1956 (mimeographed).

inadequate land utilization have not been applied.[27] True, the Geographic Institute classified almost a million hectares, mostly in areas already fairly well developed. The low cultivation quotas posed no serious problem for farmers in these areas, and even where additional classifications have been available the provisions of Decree 290 have been inoperative. A land ownership and land use questionnaire was sent out in early 1958 but answers were incomplete and of questionable validity; in any event, the results have never been tabulated. This left the government without any basic data for the effective administration of the law, and no further attempts have been made to enforce it. However, this has not discouraged Colombian policy-makers from their determination to design some kind of land tax proposal. During the last two years a number of projects incorporating a graduated land tax have been elaborated and presented to the legislature. The over-all land reform bill prepared at the end of 1960 also involves tax incentives and penalties, although it relies upon other means to reform the agrarian structure. The Colombian experience shows that little can be achieved through a land tax if there is no effective enforcement machinery.

Similar attempts have been made in other countries, notably Chile, but here again the assessment machinery has been deficient. Moreover, the law fixes the global tax base at ten times the arbitrarily calculated "rental income" of agriculture in the base year. Changes in the evaluation from year to year cannot be greater than ten times the calculated changes in "rental income" from the previous year, nor can they be negative so as to reduce assessment below that of the previous year. Rental income is estimated by a special commission, which opens the way for further manipulation of the tax base. For example, in 1957 the commission's final determination of rental income for tax assessment purposes was only about one-fourth of the total agricultural income estimated by the Chilean Development Corporation.[28]

27. Raleigh Barlowe, *Land, Taxes and Rural Economic Development in Colombia,* February 1960 (unpublished manuscript). See also *Draft Report of the FAO Regional Land Reform Team for Latin America, op. cit.*

28. Universidad de Chile, *La tributación agrícola en Chile, 1940–1958,* Instituto de Economía, Santiago, 1960.

The general impression one gets is that while the progressive land tax idea as a means of agrarian reform is theoretically attractive, in practice it runs afoul of the same power situation it is supposed to remedy. Certainly a graduated land tax cannot be easily implemented without cadastral surveys and a reasonably accurate land classification. But more importantly, there are the problems of political opposition and local enforcement which thus far have been the major obstacles to tax reform. The powerful landowning groups seem to be unwilling to submit to a graduated land tax which is of sufficient magnitude to mobilize the land market and improve the tenure distribution. By the time the balance of power has shifted away from them it is too late for such evolutionary and gradual measures and the pendulum invariably swings over to expropriation and confiscation.

NEW REFORM PROPOSALS

Plans are at present under way to introduce more or less important tenure reforms in a number of countries. Special mention should be made of projects in Peru and Colombia. A Peruvian commission on land reform and housing, which was established in President Prado's first governmental decree of August 1956, has, after four years of work, submitted the draft of a comprehensive agrarian law in September 1960.[29] Pedro Beltrán was head of the commission before he became prime minister.

The general approach of the law is a "gradualistic" one. It aims primarily at a more effective utilization of Peru's land resources and an evolutionary transformation of the land tenure system without undue disturbance. While the law provides for a large number of important measures in such fields as land and water development, colonization, the Indian communities and rural labor, it touches the problem of the present distribution of farm property most gingerly. The plantation-type irrigated estates on the coast would not, on the whole, be subject to expropriation. However, uncultivated *latifundios* in the mountain areas may be acquired by the government for redistribution. In the tropical lowlands, systematic resettlement programs are envisaged.

29. Peru, Comisión para la Reforma Agraria y la Vivienda, *La reforma agraria en el Perú* (Exposición de motivos y proyecto de ley), Talleres Gráficos Villanueva S.A., Lima, 1960.

All told, it is estimated that the law would affect approximately 25 per cent of the country's farm land, including 100,000 hectares on the coast and 3.5 million in the *sierra,* of which about half a million hectares represent land under cultivation and 3 million in natural pasture. The land would be acquired by a newly created Institute of Agrarian Reform through adequate compensation and payments over a period of five years. Land acquisition would be governed by a very complex rule, with different criteria applying to different parts of the country.

Perhaps the heart of the new law is the provision in which it assigns annually 3 per cent of the national budget to land reform over a period of ten years. Additional funds are to be made available for the opening up of new areas in the tropical lowlands and for land development in general. In this connection, it is worth mentioning that in July 1960 the Export-Import Bank and the Development Loan Fund authorized a loan of $52.5 million to Peru. Of this amount, $32.6 million is earmarked for the construction of penetration roads and $10 million for financing the establishment of colonists. A graduated land tax would produce additional revenue. The law has many other interesting provisions and is one of the most comprehensive on record. It contains 294 articles organized into 33 chapters.

Another interesting land reform project was prepared in Colombia by a special national agrarian committee in October 1960.[30] This law, the outcome of considerable social pressures and the interest of President Lleras, goes far beyond the previous taxation proposals. It declares the necessity "to reform the agrarian social structure through procedures designed to eliminate and to prevent the concentration of rural property . . . and to grant land to those who have none." The proposal would exempt from expropriation the first 300 hectares of estates, and would partially exempt an additional 500 hectares up to an absolute limit of 800. Expropriations would be made at market value, partly in cash and partly in bonds. It remains to be seen if the Peruvian and Colombian proposals will mature into law, and if so, how they will be carried out.

A most recent land reform bill was prepared by the state gov-

30. Colombia, Comité Nacional Agrario, *Proyecto de ley sobre reforma social agraria,* Bogotá, October 1960 (mimeographed).

ernment of São Paulo in Brazil and approved by the state legislature during the last days of 1960. The law provides for two types of programs: (1) subdivision and settlement of unutilized lands (giving preference to state property), and (2) creation of graduated land taxes to intensify land use. Expropriation can be effected after one year's grace if owners fail to cultivate their lands in accordance with certain criteria or to apply minimum standards to farm labor.

By the end of 1960, the following countries were reported to be considering some kind of land reform legislation and to have bills in preparation: Ecuador, Honduras, Nicaragua and Panama. An interesting plan by the state government of Buenos Aires in Argentina was shelved after the 1960 provincial elections.

CONCLUDING COMMENT

The foregoing does not pretend to cover all aspects of the complex problems of land tenure reform. Notably, policies introduced to benefit small farmers in the field of farm credit, marketing, price supports and social services have not been discussed, although many people refer to them collectively as "land reforms." It is the conviction of the writer that these and similar measures represent the focus not of land reform but of agricultural development, and that they are most effective where a healthy land tenure situation exists.

To put it in another way, land tenure improvement and agricultural development must go hand in hand. Past investments without land reforms have shown that the benefits are not shared by the large masses of farmers but go to a few big landowners and to those who monopolize the markets in farm products. Land reform without supporting measures of development — which has been the pattern so far — produces poor economic results and undue delays in raising levels of living. But on the basis of "first things first," more equitable tenure relations rate the highest priority and are a prerequisite for other types of action.

Vast land reserves are still available in Latin America for development and settlement. While the amount and accessibility of this reserve varies greatly from country to country and its quality is largely unknown, it can be said that Latin America is one of the few remaining world regions where an "agricultural frontier" still exists. Most of the frontier is in the tropical belt and the lands involved are state property.

There is a tendency to think of these new lands as the main solution for the region's land problems. Frequently it is asked: As the governments are the biggest landowners, why all the fuss about privately owned lands? True, these reserves offer opportunities to relieve the pressure in many areas, especially in the Andean highlands, where the population density is most acute. However, the public land reserves offer neither a quick enough nor a full enough solution to the present tenure problems. Experience of all countries that have settlement programs has shown that it is difficult to move large numbers of people into new areas, and that such an operation is extremely costly. Agricultural economists have repeatedly pointed out that in terms of potential production increases, the already established areas offer a much greater, more immediate and less expensive possibility. Social overhead facilities are already available in these areas which are close to the population and market centers.

This does not mean that land settlement in new zones cannot be an important factor in the agricultural development of Latin America. As a matter of fact, these new areas offer great opportunities, not only for new production, but also for the establishment of a healthier type of tenure, less encumbered by the traditional forms. Yet the colonization of far-off lands is too often used as a diversionary tactic by those who are opposed to land reforms. Settlement on public land is, of course, politically inoffensive. But even if the present rate of colonization were to be doubled or tripled, it is not likely to take the steam off the unrest and agitation in crowded areas. The bulk of the tenure problems must be resolved and the needed additional production opportunities can be found in the already settled areas.

With respect to land reform proper, the goals of tenure policy and the new institutions which would promote the frequently announced aim of economic development are only dimly visualized. The emphasis is on tearing down the old structure (principally the *latifundio* complex). Frequently there is no exploration of alternative models, beyond a vague concern with "family farming," an essentially north European and North American concept. It is doubtful, however, if the North American model in its fully commercial form is realistic for Latin America in more than a portion of the area. The medium-sized market-oriented farms in Latin American countries almost never operate with family labor alone. Even small units frequently have a *patrón* who manages and some *colonos* or *peones* who do the work.

There is little exploration of possible cooperative or communal types of tenure (the *ejido* was a very special Mexican solution). While the preoccupation with breaking up the existing system (and with it the bonds of a paternalistic and rigid class structure) may be far from wrong, there is real danger of aggravating the *minifundio* problem in the process.

Perhaps the Puerto Rican experience with what is known as the proportional-profits farms may be relevant. This arrangement is carried out under the island's Land Law of 1941. Sugar cane areas expropriated in excess of the constitutional limitation of 500 acres (applying to corporations) are operated by the Puerto Rico Land Authority, a public corporation, and farmed by unionized workers. These workers receive, in addition to their wages, part of the profits, distributed in proportion to the work done during the year. This arrangement seems to have maintained productive efficiency and is one way to distribute rights in land without excessive subdivision of the land itself. There are many possible variants of such an arrangement. The search for viable alternative tenure systems that strike an appropriate balance between social equity and productive efficiency is perhaps the most important and urgent task of land reform experts.

The preoccupation with "legalism" and with legislative details is striking. Land reform laws are invariably long, complicated and detailed. This makes their implementation very difficult. Only a fraction of the laws have actually been carried out (Bolivia is a prime example). In addition, the many detailed provisions are not only hard to implement, but are equally hard to change if they prove unworkable. The tendency to complicated laws resulted frequently in a veritable jungle of previous legislation which must be cleared away. Most of the legislative detail has of course very little meaning when it comes down to the peasants. In Bolivia, for instance, few of the illiterate Indians understand the land reform law, even though it has been translated into their native languages.

A key issue, and perhaps the most controversial one, is the expropriation procedure. With the exception of oil-rich Venezuela, no major land reform provides for acquisition of land at going market values. The exact conditions of compensation are dictated by the current conception of social justice and the relative power position of the various groups involved. Where inflation has accompanied reforms, the real value of compensation has been greatly reduced. The reforms could be placed on a self-financing basis if the landlords accepted compensation of a magnitude which was within the repayment capacity of the average beneficiary, but none of the land reforms thus far carried out has been self-financing in this sense. The basic dilemma of expropriation is how to minimize the injustices inherent in a land distribution program, which by definition goes against present market forces and pretends to change the prevailing distribution of wealth. Given overwhelming political power, a government such as Cuba seems to have no difficulty in nationalizing property. But where power is more delicately balanced, the problem of how much to pay for land and on what terms becomes more crucial.

One word about implementation. With land traditionally the basis of power, political and economic, there is an almost irresistible tendency to let personal favoritism, political influence and outright bribery intrude upon the land-granting process. The land settlement programs of most countries, on however modest a scale, have been traditionally important means for the rewarding of political favors by the ruling party. Thus land frequently does not get to the people who need it most and who are legally entitled to it. This is a further reason to justify a more drastic approach in which the peasants themselves can take an active role. Unfortunately, the framers of even revolutionary land programs seldom appreciate the necessity to make the cultivators participate actively in the land reform process. There is a tendency to manage the whole program from the top. This not only dissipates the potential contribution of the peasants to community development and self-help projects but causes great delays and frequent hardships in the distribution process itself.

It is the conclusion of this paper that, as a consequence of economic and social pressures, the central focus of land reforms in Latin America has been and will continue to be a substantial redistribution of rights in land in favor of the masses of cultivating farmers, and a corresponding shift in power and income-producing capacity. Developmental measures, such as credit, education and market assistance, must accompany tenure reforms *but are not substitutes for them.* The bulk of the reforms will take place in the already cultivated areas and will involve thorny problems of expropriation. Land settlement programs on public land and such indirect measures as land taxation can be an important complement to land tenure reforms but cannot replace them.

What are the chances for "peaceful, democratically planned reforms"? The available evidence is not encouraging. In fact, on the basis of past experience alone, an outlook of pessimism is warranted. With the possible exception of Venezuela, policy tends to polarize on one side in a "do nothing" attitude and on the other in a radical, revolutionary stance. The former group may tinker with some land settlement or tax reforms, and is likely to appoint commissions to "study the problem." It may even pass some laws — which, however, are likely to remain on the books. With this group, in general, the hope is that the problems will go away. Where, on the other hand, land reforms have been imbedded in violent revolutions, there is either a nearly complete neglect of the technical and developmental aspects (as in Bolivia) or a tendency toward political excesses (as in Cuba) which not only involve a very high social cost but may eventually cancel out the possible benefits and may even (as in Guatemala) lead to a reversal of the whole process.

Yet the picture is not without hope. An important outside factor is the future attitude and aid policy of the United States. The Act of Bogotá represents a significant new line of thinking in this respect. For the first time, an important policy document speaks of the need for "land tenure legislation and facilities with a view to ensuring a wider and more equitable distribution of the ownership of the land."[31] It is possible that the resources to be devoted to land reform under the new Special Fund for Social Development and other technical assistance will provide exceptional opportunities to support new and effective programs.

31. *Act of Bogotá* (Measures for Social Improvement and Economic Development within the Framework of Operation Pan America), in Document OEA/Ser. G/IV C-i-487, Council of the Organization of American States, November 26, 1960, p. 6.

Moreover, the spectacle of Cuba dispossessing not only the wealthy upper classes but also the middle income groups has profoundly affected the attitude of many of the ruling elements in the rest of Latin America. Meanwhile the *campesinos* have in a number of places made their voice heard, either through the ballot box (as in Chile in the last election) or, more commonly, through agitation, occupancy of *haciendas* and general rural unrest (Colombia, Peru).

This conjunction of events may eventually lead to meaningful land reform over wide areas of Latin America.